# The Collected Works
## of Olivia Ward Bush-Banks

THE SCHOMBURG LIBRARY OF
NINETEENTH-CENTURY BLACK WOMEN WRITERS

# Henry Louis Gates, Jr.
*General Editor*

Titles are listed chronologically; collections that
include works published over a span of years are listed according to
the publication date of their initial work.

Bush-Banks on left,
with Montauk relative Emma D. King on right at Indian Meeting,
Sag Harbor New York, 1931.

*The*

# Collected Works

*of*

# Olivia Ward
# Bush-Banks

*Compiled and Edited by*
BERNICE F. GUILLAUME

❧ ❧ ❧

❧ ❧ ❧

*New York   Oxford*
OXFORD UNIVERSITY PRESS
1991

Oxford University Press

Oxford   New York   Toronto
Delhi   Bombay   Calcutta   Madras   Karachi
Petaling Jaya   Singapore   Hong Kong   Tokyo
Nairobi   Dar es Salaam   Cape Town
Melbourne   Auckland

and associated companies in
Berlin   Ibadan

Library of Congress Cataloging-in-Publication Data
Bush-Banks, Olivia Ward, b. 1869.
[Works. 1991]
The collected works of Olivia Ward Bush-Banks '/
compiled and edited by Bernice F. Guillaume.
p.   cm.—(The Schomburg library of nineteenth-century Black women writers)
ISBN 0-19-506196-9
1. Afro-Americans—Literary collections.   I. Guillaume, Bernice F.
II. Title.   III. Series.
PS3503.U7644   1991
818'.409—dc20   90-36403   CIP

The
Schomburg Library
of
Nineteenth-Century
Black Women Writers
Is
Dedicated
in Memory
of
PAULINE AUGUSTA COLEMAN GATES

*1916–1987*

# PUBLISHER'S NOTE

*Whenever possible, the volumes in this set were reproduced directly from original materials. When availability, physical condition of original texts, or other circumstances prohibited this, volumes or portions of volumes were reset.*

# FOREWORD TO THE SCHOMBURG SUPPLEMENT

*Henry Louis Gates, Jr.*

The enthusiastic reception by students, scholars, and the general public to the 1988 publication of the Schomburg Library of Nineteenth-Century Black Women Writers more than justified the efforts of twenty-five scholars and the staff of the Black Periodical Literature Project to piece together the fragments of knowledge about the writings of African-American women between 1773 and 1910. The Library's republication of those writings in thirty volumes—ranging from the poetry of Phillis Wheatley to the enormous body of work that emerged out of the "Black Woman's Era" at the turn of this century—was a *beginning* for the restoration of the written sensibilities of a group of writers who confronted the twin barriers of racism and sexism in America. Through their poetry, diaries, speeches, biographies, essays, fictional narratives, and autobiographies, these writers transcended the boundaries of racial prejudice and sexual discrimination by recording the thoughts and feelings of Americans who were, at once, black *and* female. Taken together, these works configure into a literary tradition because their authors read, critiqued, and revised each other's words, in textual groundings with their sisters.

Indeed, by publishing these texts together as a "library," and by presenting them as part of a larger discourse on race and gender, we hoped to enable readers to chart the formal specificities of this tradition and to trace its origins. As a whole, the works in the Schomburg Library demonstrate that the contemporary literary movement of African-American women writers is heir to a legacy that was born in 1773, when Phillis Wheatley's *Poems on Various Subjects, Religious and Moral* first unveiled the mind of a black woman to the world. The fact that the Wheatley volume has proven to be the most popular in the Schomburg set is a testament to her role as the "founder" of both the black American's and the black woman's literary tradition.

Even before the Library was published, however, I began to receive queries about producing a supplement that would incorporate works that had not been included initially. Often these exchanges were quite dramatic. For instance, shortly before a lecture I was about to deliver at the University of Cincinnati, Professor Sharon Dean asked me if the Library would be reprinting the 1859 autobiography of Eliza Potter, a black hairdresser who had lived and worked in Cincinnati. I had never heard of Potter, I replied. Did Dean have a copy of her book? No, but there *was* a copy at the Cincinnati Historical Society. As I delivered my lecture, I could not help thinking about this "lost" text and its great significance. In fact, after the lecture, Dean and I rushed from the building and drove to the Historical Society, arriving just a few moments before closing time. A patient librarian brought us the book, and as I leafed through it, I was once again confronted with the realization that so often accompanied the research behind the Library's first thirty volumes—the exciting, yet poignant awareness that there probably exist *dozens* of works like Potter's, buried in research libraries, waiting only to be uncovered through an accident of contiguity like that which placed Sharon Dean in Cincinnati, roaming the shelves of its Historical Society. Another scholar wrote to me about work being done on the poet Effie Waller Smith. Several other scholars also wrote to share their research on other authors and their works. A supplement to the Library clearly was necessary.

Thus we have now added ten volumes, among them Potter's autobiography and Smith's collected poetry, as well as a narrative by Sojourner Truth, several pamphlets by Ida B. Wells-Barnett, and two biographies by Josephine Brown and Frances Rollin. Also included are books consisting of various essays, stories, poems, and plays whose authors did not, or could not, collect their writings into a full-length volume. The works of Olivia Ward Bush-Banks, Angelina Weld Grimké, and Katherine Davis Chapman Tillman are in this category. A related volume is an anthology of short fiction published by black women in the *Colored American Magazine* and *Crisis* magazine—a collection that reveals the shaping influence which certain periodicals had upon the generation of specific genres within the black women's literary tradition. Both types of collected books are intended to kindle an interest in still another series of works that bring together for the first time either the complete *oeuvre* of one writer or that of one genre within the periodical press. Indeed, there are several authors whose collected works will establish them as major forces in the nineteenth- and early twentieth-century black women's intellectual community. Compiling, editing, and publishing these volumes will be as important a factor in constructing the black women's literary tradition as has been the republication of books long out of print.

Finally, the Library now includes a detailed bibliography of the writings of black women in the nineteenth and early twentieth centuries. Prepared by Jean Fagan Yellin and Cynthia Bond, this bibliography is the result of years of research and will serve as an indispensable resource in future investigations of black women writers, particularly those whose works appeared frequently throughout the nineteenth century in the principal conduit of writing for black women *or* men, the African-American periodical press.

The publication of this ten-volume supplement, we hope, will make a sound contribution toward reestablishing the importance of the creative works of African-American women and reevaluating the relation of these works not only to each other but also to African-American *and* American literature and history as a whole. These works are invaluable sources for readers intent upon understanding the complex interplay of ethnicity and gender, of racism and sexism—of how "race" becomes gendered and how gender becomes racialized—in American society.

# FOREWORD
## *In Her Own Write*

### *Henry Louis Gates, Jr.*

One muffled strain in the Silent South, a jarring chord and a vague and uncomprehended cadenza has been and still is the Negro. And of that muffled chord, the one mute and voiceless note has been the sadly expectant Black Women, . . . .

The "other side" has not been represented by one who "lives there." And not many can more sensibly realize and more accurately tell the weight and the fret of the "long dull pain" than the open-eyed but hitherto voiceless Black Woman of America.

. . . as our Caucasian barristers are not to blame if they cannot *quite* put themselves in the dark man's place, neither should the dark man be wholly expected fully and adequately to reproduce the exact Voice of the Black Woman.

—ANNA JULIA COOPER
*A Voice From the South* (1892)

The birth of the African-American literary tradition occurred in 1773, when Phillis Wheatley published a book of poetry. Despite the fact that her book garnered for her a remarkable amount of attention, Wheatley's journey to the printer had been a most arduous one. Sometime in 1772, a young African girl walked demurely into a room in Boston to undergo an oral examination, the results of which would determine the direction of her life and work. Perhaps she was shocked upon entering the appointed room. For there, perhaps gathered in a semicircle, sat eighteen of Boston's most notable citizens. Among them were John Erving, a prominent Boston merchant; the Reverend Charles Chauncy, pastor of the Tenth Congregational Church; and John Hancock, who would later gain fame for his signature on the Declaration of Independence. At the center of this group was His Excellency, Thomas Hutchinson, governor of Massachusetts, with Andrew Oliver, his lieutenant governor, close by his side.

Why had this august group been assembled? Why had it seen fit to summon this young African girl, scarcely eighteen years old, before it? This group of "the most respectable Characters in *Boston*," as it would define itself, had assembled to question closely the African adolescent on the slender sheaf of poems that she claimed to have "written by herself." We can only speculate on the nature of the questions posed to the fledgling poet. Perhaps they asked her to identify and explain—for all to hear—exactly who were the Greek and Latin gods and poets alluded to so frequently in her work. Perhaps they asked her to conjugate a verb in Latin or even to translate randomly selected passages from the Latin, which she and her master, John Wheatley, claimed that she "had made some Progress in." Or perhaps they asked her to recite from memory key passages from the texts of John Milton and Alexander Pope, the two poets by whom the African claimed to be most directly influenced. We do not know.

We do know, however, that the African poet's responses were more than sufficient to prompt the eighteen august gentlemen to compose, sign, and publish a two-paragraph "Attestation," an open letter "To the Publick" that prefaces Phillis Wheatley's book and that reads in part:

> We whose Names are under-written, do assure the World, that the Poems specified in the following Page, were (as we

verily believe) written by Phillis, a young Negro Girl, who was but a few Years since, brought an uncultivated Barbarian from *Africa*, and has ever since been, and now is, under the Disadvantage of serving as a Slave in a Family in this Town. She has been examined by some of the best Judges, and is thought qualified to write them.

So important was this document in securing a publisher for Wheatley's poems that it forms the signal element in the prefatory matter preceding her *Poems on Various Subjects, Religious and Moral,* published in London in 1773.

Without the published "Attestation," Wheatley's publisher claimed, few would believe that an African could possibly have written poetry all by herself. As the eighteen put the matter clearly in their letter, "Numbers would be ready to suspect they were not really the Writings of Phillis." Wheatley and her master, John Wheatley, had attempted to publish a similar volume in 1772 in Boston, but Boston publishers had been incredulous. One year later, "Attestation" in hand, Phillis Wheatley and her master's son, Nathaniel Wheatley, sailed for England, where they completed arrangements for the publication of a volume of her poems with the aid of the Countess of Huntington and the Earl of Dartmouth.

This curious anecdote, surely one of the oddest oral examinations on record, is only a tiny part of a larger, and even more curious, episode in the Enlightenment. Since the beginning of the sixteenth century, Europeans had wondered aloud whether or not the African "species of men," as they were most commonly called, *could* ever create formal literature, could ever master "the arts and sciences." If they could, the argument ran, then the African variety of humanity was fundamentally related to the European variety. If not, then it seemed clear that the African was destined by nature to be a slave. This was the burden shouldered by Phillis Wheatley when she successfully defended herself and the authorship of her book against counterclaims and doubts.

Indeed, with her successful defense, Wheatley launched two traditions at once—the black American literary tradition *and* the black woman's literary tradition. If it is extraordinary that not just one but both of these traditions were founded simultaneously by a black woman—certainly an event unique in the history of literature—it is also ironic that this important fact of common, coterminous literary origins seems to have escaped most scholars.

That the progenitor of the black literary tradition was a woman means, in the most strictly literal sense, that all subsequent black writers have evolved in a matrilinear line of descent, and that each, consciously or unconsciously, has extended and revised a canon whose foundation was the poetry of a black woman. Early black writers seem to have been keenly aware of Wheatley's founding role, even if most of her white reviewers were more concerned with the implications of her race than her gender. Jupiter Hammon, for example, whose 1760 broadside "An Evening Thought. Salvation by Christ, With Penitential Cries" was the first individual poem published by a black American, acknowledged Wheatley's influence by selecting her as the subject of his second broadside, "An Address to Miss Phillis Wheatly [*sic*], Ethiopian Poetess, in Boston," which was published in Hartford in 1778. And George Moses Horton, the second African American to publish a book of poetry in English (1829), brought out in 1838 an edition of his *Poems By A Slave* bound together with Wheatley's work. Indeed, for fifty-six years, between 1773 and 1829, when Horton published *The Hope of Liberty*, Wheatley was the *only* black person to have published a book of imaginative literature in English. So central was this black woman's role in the shaping of the

African-American literary tradition that, as one historian has maintained, the history of the reception of Phillis Wheatley's poetry *is* the history of African-American literary criticism. Well into the nineteenth century, Wheatley and the black literary tradition were the same entity.

But Wheatley is not the only black woman writer who stands as a pioneering figure in African-American literature. Just as Wheatley gave birth to the genre of black poetry, Ann Plato was the first African American to publish a book of essays (1841) and Harriet E. Wilson was the first black person to publish a novel in the United States (1859).

Despite this pioneering role of black women in the tradition, however, many of their contributions before this century have been all but lost or unrecognized. As Hortense Spillers observed as recently as 1983,

> With the exception of a handful of autobiographical narratives from the nineteenth century, the black woman's realities are virtually suppressed until the period of the Harlem Renaissance and later. Essentially the black woman as artist, as intellectual spokesperson for her own cultural apprenticeship, has not existed before, for anyone. At the source of [their] own symbol-making task, [the community of black women writers] confronts, therefore, a tradition of work that is quite recent, its continuities, broken and sporadic.

Until now, it has been extraordinarily difficult to establish the formal connections between early black women's writing and that of the present, precisely because our knowledge of their work has been broken and sporadic. Phillis Wheatley, for example, while certainly the most reprinted and discussed poet in the tradition, is also one of the least understood. Ann Plato's seminal work, *Essays* (which includes biographies and poems), has not been reprinted since it was published a century and a half ago. And Harriet Wilson's *Our Nig*, her

compelling novel of a black woman's expanding consciousness in a racist Northern antebellum environment, never received even *one* review or comment at a time when virtually
*all* works written by black people were heralded by abolition-
ists as salient arguments against the existence of human slavery. Many of the books reprinted in this set experienced a
similar fate, the most dreadful fate for an author: that of
being ignored then relegated to the obscurity of the rare book
section of a university library. We can only wonder how
many other texts in the black woman's tradition have been
lost to this generation of readers or remain unclassified or
uncatalogued and, hence, unread.

This was not always so, however. Black women writers
dominated the final decade of the nineteenth century, perhaps
spurred to publish by an 1886 essay entitled "The Coming
American Novelist," which was published in *Lippincott's
Monthly Magazine* and written by "A Lady From Philadelphia." This pseudonymous essay argued that the "Great
American Novel" would be written by a black person. Her
argument is so curious that it deserves to be repeated:

> When we come to formulate our demands of the Coming
> American Novelist, we will agree that he must be native-
> born. His ancestors may come from where they will, but we
> must give him a birthplace and have the raising of him.
> Still, the longer his family has been here the better he will
> represent us. Suppose he should have no country but ours,
> no traditions but those he has learned here, no longings apart
> from us, no future except in our future—the orphan of the
> world, he finds with us his home. And with all this, suppose
> he refuses to be fused into that grand conglomerate we call
> the "American type." With us, he is not of us. He is origi-
> nal, he has humor, he is tender, he is passive and fiery, he
> has been taught what we call justice, and he has his own
> opinion about it. He has suffered everything a poet, a dra-

matist, a novelist need suffer before he comes to have his lips
anointed. And with it all he is in one sense a spectator, a
little out of the race. How would these conditions go towards
forming an original development? In a word, suppose the
coming novelist is of African origin? When one comes to
consider the subject, there is no improbability in it. One
thing is certain,—our great novel will not be written by the
typical American.

An atypical American, indeed. Not only would the great
American novel be written by an African American, it would
be written by an African-American *woman:*

> Yet farther: I have used the generic masculine pronoun be-
> cause it is convenient; but Fate keeps revenge in store. It was
> a woman who, taking the wrongs of the African as her theme,
> wrote the novel that awakened the world to their reality, and
> why should not the coming novelist be a woman as well as
> an African? She—the woman of that race—has some claims
> on Fate which are not yet paid up.

It is these claims on fate that we seek to pay by publishing
The Schomburg Library of Nineteenth-Century Black Women
Writers.

This theme would be repeated by several black women
authors, most notably by Anna Julia Cooper, a prototypical
black feminist whose 1892 *A Voice From the South* can be
considered to be one of the original texts of the black feminist
movement. It was Cooper who first analyzed the fallacy of
referring to "the Black man" when speaking of black people
and who argued that just as white men cannot speak through
the consciousness of black men, neither can black *men* "fully
and adequately . . . reproduce the exact Voice of the Black
Woman." Gender and race, she argues, cannot be conflated,
except in the instance of a black woman's voice, and it is this
voice which must be uttered and to which we must listen. As
Cooper puts the matter so compellingly:

It is not the intelligent woman vs. the ignorant woman; nor the white woman vs. the black, the brown, and the red,—it is not even the cause of woman vs. man. Nay, 'tis woman's strongest vindication for speaking that *the world needs to hear her voice*. It would be subversive of every human interest that the cry of one-half the human family be stifled. Woman in stepping from the pedestal of statue-like inactivity in the domestic shrine, and daring to think and move and speak,—to undertake to help shape, mold, and direct the thought of her age, is merely completing the circle of the world's vision. Hers is every interest that has lacked an interpreter and a defender. Her cause is linked with that of every agony that has been dumb—every wrong that needs a voice.

It is no fault of man's that he has not been able to see truth from her standpoint. It does credit both to his head and heart that no greater mistakes have been committed or even wrongs perpetrated while she sat making tatting and snipping paper flowers. Man's own innate chivalry and the mutual interdependence of their interests have insured his treating her cause, in the main at least, as his own. And he is pardonably surprised and even a little chagrined, perhaps, to find his legislation not considered "perfectly lovely" in every respect. But in any case his work is only impoverished by her remaining dumb. The world has had to limp along with the wobbling gait and one-sided hesitancy of a man with one eye. Suddenly the bandage is removed from the other eye and the whole body is filled with light. It sees a circle where before it saw a segment. The darkened eye restored, every member rejoices with it.

The myopic sight of the darkened eye can only be restored when the full range of the black woman's voice, with its own special timbres and shadings, remains mute no longer.

Similarly, Victoria Earle Matthews, an author of short stories and essays, and a cofounder in 1896 of the National Association of Colored Women, wrote in her stunning essay,

"The Value of Race Literature" (1895), that "when the literature of our race is developed, it will of necessity be different in all essential points of greatness, true heroism and real Christianity from what we may at the present time, for convenience, call American literature." Matthews argued that this great tradition of African-American literature would be the textual outlet "for the unnaturally suppressed inner lives which our people have been compelled to lead." Once these "unnaturally suppressed inner lives" of black people are unveiled, no "grander diffusion of mental light" will shine more brightly, she concludes, than that of the articulate African-American woman:

> And now comes the question, What part shall we women play in the Race Literature of the future? . . . within the compass of one small journal ["Woman's Era"] we have struck out a new line of departure—a journal, a record of Race interests gathered from all parts of the United States, carefully selected, moistened, winnowed and garnered by the ablest intellects of educated colored women, shrinking at no lofty theme, shirking no serious duty, aiming at every possible excellence, and determined to do their part in the future uplifting of the race.
>
> If twenty women, by their concentrated efforts in one literary movement, can meet with such success as has engendered, planned out, and so successfully consummated this convention, what much more glorious results, what wider spread success, what grander diffusion of mental light will not come forth at the bidding of the enlarged hosts of women writers, already called into being by the stimulus of your efforts?
>
> And here let me speak one word for my journalistic sisters who have already entered the broad arena of journalism. Before the "Woman's Era" had come into existence, no one except themselves can appreciate the bitter experience and sore

disappointments under which they have at all times been compelled to pursue their chosen vocations.

If their brothers of the press have had their difficulties to contend with, I am here as a sister journalist to state, from the fullness of knowledge, that their task has been an easy one compared with that of the colored woman in journalism.

Woman's part in Race Literature, as in Race building, is the most important part and has been so in all ages. . . . All through the most remote epochs she has done her share in literature. . . .

One of the most important aspects of this set is the republication of the salient texts from 1890 to 1910, which literary historians could well call the "Black Woman's Era." In addition to Mary Helen Washington's definitive edition of Cooper's *A Voice From the South,* we have reprinted two novels by Amelia Johnson, Frances Harper's *Iola Leroy,* two novels by Emma Dunham Kelley, Alice Dunbar-Nelson's two impressive collections of short stories, and Pauline Hopkins's three serialized novels as well as her monumental novel, *Contending Forces*—all published between 1890 and 1910. Indeed, black women published more works of fiction in these two decades than black men had published in the previous half century. Nevertheless, this great achievement has been ignored.

Moreover, the writings of nineteenth-century African-American women in general have remained buried in obscurity, accessible only in research libraries or in overpriced and poorly edited reprints. Many of these books have never been reprinted at all; in some instances only one or two copies are extant. In these works of fiction, poetry, autobiography, biography, essays, and journalism resides the mind of the nineteenth-century African-American woman. Until these works are made readily available to teachers and their students, a significant segment of the black tradition will remain silent.

Oxford University Press, in collaboration with the Schomburg Center for Research in Black Culture, is publishing thirty volumes of these compelling works, each of which contains an introduction by an expert in the field. The set includes such rare texts as Johnson's *The Hazeley Family* and *Clarence and Corinne,* Plato's *Essays,* the most complete edition of Phillis Wheatley's poems and letters, Emma Dunham Kelley's pioneering novel *Megda,* several previously unpublished stories and a novel by Alice Dunbar-Nelson, and the first collected volumes of Pauline Hopkins's three serialized novels and Frances Harper's poetry. We also present four volumes of poetry by such women as Henrietta Cordelia Ray, Adah Menken, Josephine Heard, and Maggie Johnson. Numerous slave and spiritual narratives, a newly discovered novel—*Four Girls at Cottage City*—by Emma Dunham Kelley (-Hawkins), and the first American edition of *Wonderful Adventures of Mrs. Seacole in Many Lands* are also among the texts included.

In addition to resurrecting the works of black women authors, it is our hope that this set will facilitate the resurrection of the African-American woman's literary tradition itself by unearthing its nineteenth-century roots. In the works of Nella Larsen and Jessie Fauset, Zora Neale Hurston and Ann Petry, Lorraine Hansberry and Gwendolyn Brooks, Paule Marshall and Toni Cade Bambara, Audre Lorde and Rita Dove, Toni Morrison and Alice Walker, Gloria Naylor and Jamaica Kincaid, these roots have branched luxuriantly. The eighteenth- and nineteenth-century authors whose works are presented in this set founded and nurtured the black women's literary tradition, which must be revived, explicated, analyzed, and debated before we can understand more completely the formal shaping of this tradition within a tradition, a coded literary universe through which, regrettably, we are only just beginning to navigate our way. As Anna Cooper said nearly one hundred years ago, we have been blinded by the loss of sight in one eye and have therefore been unable to detect the full *shape* of the African-American literary tradition.

Literary works configure into a tradition not because of some mystical collective unconscious determined by the biology of race or gender, but because writers read other writers and *ground* their representations of experience in models of language provided largely by other writers to whom they feel akin. It is through this mode of literary revision, amply evident in the *texts* themselves—in formal echoes, recast metaphors, even in parody—that a "tradition" emerges and defines itself.

This is formal bonding, and it is only through formal bonding that we can know a literary tradition. The collective publication of these works by black women now, for the first time, makes it possible for scholars and critics, male and female, black and white, to *demonstrate* that black women writers read, and revised, other black women writers. To demonstrate this set of formal literary relations is to demonstrate that sexuality, race, and gender are both the condition and the basis of *tradition*—but tradition as found in discrete acts of language use.

A word is in order about the history of this set. For the past decade, I have taught a course, first at Yale and then at Cornell, entitled "Black Woman and Their Fictions," a course that I inherited from Toni Morrison, who developed it in the mid-1970s for Yale's Program in Afro-American Studies. Although the course was inspired by the remarkable accomplishments of black women novelists since 1970, I gradually extended its beginning date to the late nineteenth century, studying Frances Harper's *Iola Leroy* and Anna Julia Cooper's *A Voice From the South*, both published in 1892. With the discovery of Harriet E. Wilson's seminal novel, *Our Nig* (1859), and Jean Yellin's authentication of Harriet Jacobs's brilliant slave narrative, *Incidents in the Life of a Slave Girl* (1861), a survey course spanning over a century and a quarter emerged.

But the discovery of *Our Nig*, as well as the interest in nineteenth-century black women's writing that this discovery generated, convinced me that even the most curious and diligent scholars knew very little of the extensive history of the creative writings of African-American women before 1900. Indeed, most scholars of African-American literature had never even read most of the books published by black women, simply because these books—of poetry, novels, short stories, essays, and autobiography—were mostly accessible only in rare book sections of university libraries. For reasons unclear to me even today, few of these marvelous renderings of the African-American woman's consciousness were reprinted in the late 1960s and early 1970s, when so many other texts of the African-American literary tradition were resurrected from the dark and silent graveyard of the out-of-print and were reissued in facsimile editions aimed at the hungry readership for canonical texts in the nascent field of black studies.

So, with the help of several superb research assistants—including David Curtis, Nicola Shilliam, Wendy Jones, Sam Otter, Janadas Devan, Suvir Kaul, Cynthia Bond, Elizabeth Alexander, and Adele Alexander—and with the expert advice of scholars such as William Robinson, William Andrews, Mary Helen Washington, Maryemma Graham, Jean Yellin, Houston A. Baker, Jr., Richard Yarborough, Hazel Carby, Joan R. Sherman, Frances Foster, and William French, dozens of bibliographies were used to compile a list of books written or narrated by black women mostly before 1910. Without the assistance provided through this shared experience of scholarship, the scholar's true legacy, this project would not have been conceived. As the list grew, I was struck by how very many of these titles that I, for example, had never even heard of, let alone read, such as Ann Plato's *Essays*, Louisa Picquet's slave narrative, or Amelia Johnson's two novels, *Clarence and Corinne* and *The Hazeley Family*. Through our research with the Black Periodical Fiction and Poetry Project (funded by NEH and the Ford Foundation), I also realized that several novels by black women, including three works of fiction by Pauline Hopkins, had been serialized in black periodicals, but had never been collected and published as books. Nor had the several books of poetry published by black women, such as the prolific Frances E. W. Harper, been collected and edited. When I discovered still another "lost" novel by an African-American woman (*Four Girls at Cottage City*, published in 1898 by Emma Dunham Kelley-Hawkins), I decided to attempt to edit a collection of reprints of these works and to publish them as a "library" of black women's writings, in part so that I could read them myself.

Convincing university and trade publishers to undertake this project proved to be a difficult task. Despite the commercial success of *Our Nig* and of the several reprint series of women's works (such as Virago, the Beacon Black Women Writers Series, and Rutgers' American Women Writers Series), several presses rejected the project as "too large," "too limited," or as "commercially unviable." Only two publishers recognized the viability and the import of the project and, of these, Oxford's commitment to publish the titles simultaneously as a set made the press's offer irresistible.

While attempting to locate original copies of these exceedingly rare books, I discovered that most of the texts were housed at the Schomburg Center for Research in Black Culture, a branch of The New York Public Library, under the direction of Howard Dodson. Dodson's infectious enthusiasm for the project and his generous collaboration, as well as that of his stellar staff (especially Diana Lachatanere, Sharon Howard, Ellis Haizip, Richard Newman, and Betty Gubert), led to a joint publishing initiative that produced this set as part of the Schomburg's major fund-raising campaign. Without Dodson's foresight and generosity of spirit, the set would not have materialized. Without William P. Sisler's masterful editorship at Oxford and his staff's careful attention to detail, the set would have remained just another grand idea that tends to languish in a scholar's file cabinet.

I would also like to thank Dr. Michael Winston and Dr. Thomas C. Battle, Vice-President of Academic Affairs and the Director of the Moorland-Spingarn Research Center (respectively) at Howard University, for their unending encouragement, support, and collaboration in this project, and Esme E. Bhan at Howard for her meticulous research and bibliographical skills. In addition, I would like to acknowledge the aid of the staff at the libraries of Duke University, Cornell University (especially Tom Weissinger and Donald Eddy), the Boston Public Library, the Western Reserve Historical Society, the Library of Congress, and Yale University. Linda Robbins, Marion Osmun, Sarah Flanagan, and Gerard Case, all members of the staff at Oxford, were extraordinarily effective at coordinating, editing, and producing the various segments of each text in the set. Candy Ruck, Nina de Tar, and Phillis Molock expertly typed reams of correspondence and manuscripts connected to the project.

I would also like to express my gratitude to my colleagues who edited and introduced the individual titles in the set. Without their attention to detail, their willingness to meet strict deadlines, and their sheer enthusiasm for this project, the set could not have been published. But finally and ultimately, I would hope that the publication of the set would help to generate even more scholarly interest in the black women authors whose work is presented here. Struggling against the seemingly insurmountable barriers of racism *and* sexism, while often raising families and fulfilling full-time professional obligations, these women managed nevertheless to record their thoughts and feelings and to *testify* to all who dare read them that the will to harness the power of collective endurance and survival is the will to write.

The Schomburg Library of Nineteenth-Century Black Women Writers is dedicated in memory of Pauline Augusta Coleman Gates, who died in the spring of 1987. It was she who inspired in me the love of learning and the love of literature. I have encountered in the books of this set no will more determined, no courage more noble, no mind more sublime, no self more celebratory of the achievements of all African-American women, and indeed of life itself, than her own.

# A NOTE FROM
# THE SCHOMBURG CENTER

*Howard Dodson*

The Schomburg Center for Research in Black Culture, The New York Public Library, is pleased to join with Dr. Henry Louis Gates and Oxford University Press in presenting The Schomburg Library of Nineteenth-Century Black Women Writers. This thirty-volume set includes the work of a generation of black women whose writing has only been available previously in rare book collections. The materials reprinted in twenty-four of the thirty volumes are drawn from the unique holdings of the Schomburg Center.

A research unit of The New York Public Library, the Schomburg Center has been in the forefront of those institutions dedicated to collecting, preserving, and providing access to the records of the black past. In the course of its two generations of acquisition and conservation activity, the Center has amassed collections totaling more than 5 million items. They include over 100,000 bound volumes, 85,000 reels and sets of microforms, 300 manuscript collections containing some 3.5 million items, 300,000 photographs and extensive holdings of prints, sound recordings, film and videotape, newspapers, artworks, artifacts, and other book and nonbook materials. Together they vividly document the history and cultural heritages of people of African descent worldwide.

Though established some sixty-two years ago, the Center's book collections date from the sixteenth century. Its oldest item, an Ethiopian Coptic Tunic, dates from the eighth or ninth century. Rare materials, however, are most available for the nineteenth-century African-American experience. It is from these holdings that the majority of the titles selected for inclusion in this set are drawn.

The nineteenth century was a formative period in African-American literary and cultural history. Prior to the Civil War, the majority of black Americans living in the United States were held in bondage. Law and practice forbade teaching them to read or write. Even after the war, many of the impediments to learning and literary productivity remained. Nevertheless, black men and women of the nineteenth century persevered in both areas. Moreover, more African Americans than we yet realize turned their observations, feelings, social viewpoints, and creative impulses into published works. In time, this nineteenth-century printed record included poetry, short stories, histories, novels, autobiographies, social criticism, and theology, as well as economic and philosophical treatises. Unfortunately, much of this body of literature remained, until very recently, relatively inaccessible to twentieth-century scholars, teachers, creative artists, and others interested in black life. Prior to the late 1960s, most Americans (black as well as white) had never heard of these nineteenth-century authors, much less read their works.

The civil rights and black power movements created unprecedented interest in the thought, behavior, and achievements of black people. Publishers responded by revising traditional texts, introducing the American public to a new generation of African-American writers, publishing a variety of thematic anthologies, and reprinting a plethora of "classic texts" in African-American history, literature, and art. The reprints usually appeared as individual titles or in a series of bound volumes or microform formats.

The Schomburg Center, which has a long history of supporting publishing that deals with the history and culture of Africans in diaspora, became an active participant in many of the reprint revivals of the 1960s. Since hard copies of original printed works are the preferred formats for producing facsimile reproductions, publishers frequently turned to the Schomburg Center for copies of these original titles. In addition to providing such material, Schomburg Center staff members offered advice and consultation, wrote introductions, and occasionally entered into formal copublishing arrangements in some projects.

Most of the nineteenth-century titles reprinted during the 1960s, however, were by and about black men. A few black women were included in the longer series, but works by lesser known black women were generally overlooked. The Schomburg Library of Nineteenth-Century Black Women Writers is both a corrective to these previous omissions and an important contribution to African-American literary history in its own right. Through this collection of volumes, the thoughts, perspectives, and creative abilities of nineteenth-century African-American women, as captured in books and pamphlets published in large part before 1910, are again being made available to the general public. The Schomburg Center is pleased to be a part of this historic endeavor.

I would like to thank Professor Gates for initiating this project. Thanks are due both to him and Mr. William P. Sisler of Oxford University Press for giving the Schomburg Center an opportunity to play such a prominent role in the set. Thanks are also due to my colleagues at The New York Public Library and the Schomburg Center, especially Dr. Vartan Gregorian, Richard De Gennaro, Paul Fasana, Betsy Pinover, Richard Newman, Diana Lachatanere, Glenderlyn Johnson, and Harold Anderson for their assistance and support. I can think of no better way of demonstrating than in this set the role the Schomburg Center plays in assuring that the black heritage will be available for future generations.

# CONTENTS

PLAYS, VIGNETTES, ESSAYS, SKETCHES

This volume is dedicated
to the memory of Esther Washington Smith,
a loyal descendant of Montauk.

# The Collected Works
## of Olivia Ward Bush-Banks

# INTRODUCTION

*Bernice F. Guillaume*

How would one characterize an "African Indian"? In the harsh glare of the post-1960s black revolution, the concept may seem bizarre or even ludicrous. Yet from this ethnic combination on eastern Long Island, New York, emerged an extraordinary woman and writer, Olivia Ward Bush-Banks (1869–1944). In many respects she paralleled her contemporaries in the style and content of black America's *fin du siècle* literature. But in other ways she was unique. Through several poems and a play, she spoke expressly to the Native American experience and helped preserve fragments of the Montauk tribe's language and folklore. She maintained a lifelong observance of annual Indian meetings and "pow-wows." Several of her works even disclose Bahai and socialist influences. In sum, she represented a living anachronism of assimilation and transculturalization on North America's eastern seaboard.

At the same time, Bush-Banks was proud of her African heritage. This self-esteem was apparent in a wide range of genres—including poetry, plays, dramatic monologues, short stories, sketches, and essays—and in social activism. Her plays were often didactic or satiric, devices she used to illustrate both the positive and negative qualities of African-American society and of human nature in general.

Unlike most African Americans knowledgeable of their Amer-Indian ancestry, Bush-Banks embraced and consciously cultivated her dual sensibility. It is a sensibility that challenges traditional ethnic categorization and that clouds an objective understanding and analysis of her use of tone, meaning, and figurative language. This essay thus attempts to shed light on an enigmatic and complex woman of color.

A narrative on Bush-Banks's early years is found in an autobiographical statement inserted in the Brown University copy of her 1914 collection of poetry and prose, *Driftwood*.[1] She was born to Abraham and Eliza Draper Ward in Sag Harbor, New York. Following the death of her mother in November 1869 and the remarriage of her father, Bush-Banks was raised by her aunt, Maria (pronounced Mo-ri-a) Draper, in Providence, Rhode Island. Bush-Banks attended Providence High School, where she developed an affinity for drama and literature. In a cryptic note she relates:

> Background training for Behavior Drama—Providence (Rhode Island) High School (2nd year literature), instructed by Miss Dodge (Dramatic Director of Dodge School of Dramatics). Knowledge of Behavior Drama began with Samuel Taylor Coleridge's *Ancient Mariner,* Miss Dodge insisting upon emotional behavior in its interpretation. I was called upon to demonstrate whenever Supt. [Superintendent] or official of schools visited class. I interpreted "eagerness of Ancient Mariner" to tell his experience: "loneliness on the wide, wide sea, longing for water, surrounded by sea and not a drop to drink." Miss Dodge became interested and gave me private lessons after each period during that year.[2]

In spite of her technical training as a seamstress, Bush-Banks's early contact with the artistic world would forever color her life. But she was not ungrateful for an industrial education, praising her aunt's sacrifices on her behalf:

> Through her [Maria's] efforts I have secured a useful, practical education, and firmly believe that whatever I have attained . . . is due to her untiring zeal and loving interest in

my welfare. She also exercised that same zeal and interest throughout that portion of my life which proved most extremely unfortunate.[3]

This "extremely unfortunate" period was Bush-Banks's first marriage in 1889 to Frank Bush, a tailor from Columbia, South Carolina. The marriage was over by 1895, and Bush-Banks became the sole provider for herself and her two daughters, Rosa Olivia (Rosamund) and Marie. From the late 1890s to about 1916, she alternated living between Boston and Providence and took any menial job available in a region reeling under the impact of the second Industrial Revolution.

Surrounded by hardship, Bush-Banks turned to her love of poetry and dramatics for emotional and financial support. The result was her first volume, *Original Poems* (1899). The work enjoyed a small degree of success, and several selections were reprinted in the *Boston Transcript* and the *Voice of the Negro*. But caring for her dependents—which now included her aunt, as well as her two daughters—meant postponing a full-time writing career. Bush-Banks's interim state of mind is illustrated by excerpts from her 1912 letter to the writer and spiritualist Ella Wheeler Wilcox:

> For about fifteen years I have been desirous of publishing a collection of prose and verses . . . [because] I have tasted the cup of human sorrow and disappointment, and I feel that I ought to be helpful to others for this very reason.
>
> . . . . I have let go my hold somehow on the hopefulness of former days; I have lost my way. . . .
>
> Oh, I am so heart-hungry for mental encouragement, I need your strength, and again I ask you to give me your best thought for my heart's desire.[4]

Bush-Banks's autobiographical statement also highlights her dual ancestry:

> I seemed to have lost my identity regarding the distinctness
> of race, being of African and Indian descent. Both parents
> possessed some negro blood, and were also descendants of the
> Montauk tribe of Indians, which tribe formerly occupied the
> eastern end of Long Island known as Montauk.[5]

Bush-Banks hints that her aunt was responsible for instilling
a Native American ethos. But the crucial difference between
Bush-Banks and most other blacks who shared Indian descent
lay in the former's *conscious* immersion in an Algonquian
heritage.

To a certain extent her Native American fidelity was a
product of the times. She grew up in an era when Long
Island's mixed-blood Native American descendants, as well
as other mixed-bloods throughout the eastern seaboard, were
fighting to retain their legal and social identities. That she
emphasized the Indian side of the African equation was thus
not an effort to escape discrimination. The New York State
Supreme Court case *Wyandanch Pharoah v. Jane Ann Benson
and Others* (1910) rendered the Montauk tribe legally ex-
tinct. A deluge of appeals heightened mixed-bloods' pan-
Indian sentiments and generated unity among the rival Eastville and Freetown Montauk tribal factions. Additionally,
Nathan J. Cuffee, a blind Montauk from the tribe's Eastville
(Sag Harbor) faction, and Lydia Jocelyn, the wife of a Da-
kota Sioux missionary, co-authored a historical novel of early
Anglo-Montauk relations, titled *Lords of the Soil* (1909). The
work was one more indication of the mixed-bloods' determination to maintain their identity.[6]

The struggle over the status of the Poosepatuck Indian
(Unkechaug people) reservation school in Mastic, New York,
was another mixed-blood battleground. The institution was
one of the first missionary outposts of the Presbyterian Church
in the United States, but between the 1880s and 1930s it was

caught in a tug-of-war between state financing authorities and clergy-administrators. Ultimately the school lost its funding because the former considered the tribal lands more of a "plantation" than a "reservation." Still, the school provided a rudimentary education for many reservation children, including the Wards, who were among the oldest Poosepatuck families. Bush-Banks's uncle, Jacob Ward, had a permanent homestead on the reservation, and Wards held the position of *sachem* (chief) at Poosepatuck from the early nineteenth century to the 1930s.[7]

Given these attacks on her cultural integrity, it is no surprise that throughout her adult life Bush-Banks attended pow-wows and other native gatherings on Long Island. Her memorabilia include a 1931 photograph of herself and a Native American relative, Emma Depth, in tribal regalia during that year's Indian meeting in Sag Harbor. The existing fragments from Bush-Banks's unpublished play *Indian Trails; or, Trail of the Montauk* (c. 1920) show character roles matching Algonquian social and cultural patterns, and names that correspond to the *r* Algonquian dialect traditionally existing between eastern Long Island and southeastern New England.

Interviews with residents of the Shinnecock and Poosepatuck reservations in Southampton and Mastic, New York, respectively, have affirmed Bush-Banks's blood ties to those peoples.[8] In addition, prior to 1916 Bush-Banks served as the Montauk tribal historian.[9]

But Bush-Banks valued her African roots as well. She saw herself as a "colored" person in a *nineteenth-century* context—one who was either black or a mixture of African and Native American. Her protest poetry and essays mirror her acceptance of an official, if inaccurate, social categorization as an African American. But a clearly extant cultural niche in Bush-

Banks's time is not necessarily comprehensible to contemporary critics, especially those standing outside the African-Indians' world.

Other sources inform us of Bush-Banks's long career. John Daniels mentions her as a settlement house activist in his 1914 work *In Freedom's Birthplace: A Study of the Boston Negroes*.[10] Furthermore, between 1900 and 1904, she contributed to the *Colored American Magazine* and was active in the Northeastern Federation of Womens' Clubs. Her personal papers divulge her stint as literary editor of Boston's *Citizen* magazine.

Her memorabilia also shed light on her life in Chicago from about 1916 to about 1928, a period during which she married a Pullman porter named Anthony Banks, found kindred spirits among Chicago's Lincoln Center artists, and established a drama school:

> Chicago: Close contact with Moffatt school of Expression, which specialized in English and Dramatic Interpretation. Became convinced that Behavior Drama was a special foundation for instructing children, I opened Bush-Banks School of Expression at my studio, giving instructions after school and Saturdays. As a result was employed in the public schools, Willard School Community Evenings. Attendance as high as 30 or 40 children, teaching them emotional values, appointing individual groups of children to create and interpret their choice of Dramatic subjects.
>
> Also taught Summer Season in Mosely School . . . also Community Evening at John Farren School.[11]

Clippings from a July 1931 issue of the *Chicago Defender*, as well as from the (New York) *Interstate Tattler* (27 June 1930) and the Rand School of Social Science *Notes* (18 May 1933), indicate she resided intermittently between Chicago and New York from the 1920s to the 1930s. From her art studios in both cities, she hosted dramatic renditions by herself and others, as well as music recitals and other intellectual *soirées*. In addition, she was active in the Works Progress (Project) Administration in New York:

> In 1936 I was appointed by the WPA Community Drama Unit to demonstrate Behavior Drama at Adam Powell's Abyssinia Community Center for 3 years. Later, in small churches (also with adult groups who aspired to business, millinery, etc.), giving them Behavior procedure in salesmanship. Dr. Simm's church, 145th Street; Dramatic director (Behavior Plays); Rev. Mr. [Mc?] Licorish church (152nd St.), Ebenezer Baptist Church, 313 W. 141st St.
>
> Extension instruction in dramatics: WPA, nearly 8 weeks' course in Theatre Techniques at Provincetown Studio Theatre, 133 Macdougal Street (including designing costumes, scenic props, stage effects, lighting, makeup, Community Drama, stage areas, speech construction). Also 12 lesson courses at N.Y. University under Prof. Roy Mitchell, and also at Roerrich Hall, Riverside Drive.[12]

Her papers contain a certificate of completion, dated January 1936, in the teacher education program for theater from the Division of General Education at New York University's Adult Education Project.

Bush-Banks's papers clearly show that in spite of limited resources she was a patron of the New Negro movement. Clippings from the early 1930s feature her as the "Cultural Art" columnist for the (New Rochelle) *Westchester Record-Courier*. From this platform she applauded the works of Richmond Barthe, Langston Hughes, and other African-American artists. In personal interviews Barthe recalled knowing Bush-Banks well. Elizabeth Bowser, granddaughter of T. Thomas Fortune, editor of the *New York Age*, remembered Bush-Banks as a well-known Harlem figure who once lived in an apartment above the Fortunes.[13] Additionally, Carter G. Woodson, editor of the *Negro History Bulletin,* wrote to Bush-Banks in December 1938, noting "I have received your poetry and I like it very much."[14] Interviews with Bush-Banks's descendants, and a glance at her unpublished memoirs, *The Lure of the Distances* (c. 1935–1944), show that she cultivated friendships from a wide variety of ethnic groups.[15] In sum, she emerges as a minor but viable elder of the Negro Renaissance movement.

An overview of Bush-Banks's published and unpublished writings discloses the pride she felt in her African- and Native American heritage. By virtue of her lengthy career and the years it encompassed, her works also illustrate the literary, ethnic, and socioeconomic transitions reshaping the United States between the late nineteenth century and World War II.

*Original Poems* exhibits the lingering influences of neoclassic literary forms and devices as well as the prevalence of such Fireside Poets as J. G. Whittier, W. C. Bryant, and H. W. Longfellow. The volume particularly reflects Whittier's advocacy of a literature containing "the spontaneous outgushings of hearts warm with love," and Byrant's insistence that poetry be a medium for "moral uplift and spiritual refinement."[16]

Two elegies, four odes, and four nature/religious poems complete the volume. The only obvious thematic unity is the opening and closing selections, "Morning on Shinnecock" and "Voices." They share hill settings and first-person speakers; they commence and end the collection on the despairing and hopeful sentiments that reflect the late nineteenth-century's social climate.

Moreover, "Morning on Shinnecock" underlines Bush-Banks's African-Indian duality. In this poem, dawn on the central hill at the Shinnecock reservation provides a metaphor for Bush-Banks's reflections on happier times. The sweeter early years have yielded to the harsh glare of life: "But, merging into sorrow's day,/ then beauty faded with the morn." Likewise, the turn of the century foreshadowed heightened battles between the town of Southampton and the Shinnecocks over the retention of their ancestral lands. The poem shows the romantic's yearning for a world refashioned by personal desires. It also expresses the apprehension shared by both Native and African Americans at the dawn of an oppressive new century.

Sometimes Bush-Banks utilized a modified English sonnet for brooding introspection; as in "Voices," which was later reprinted in *Driftwood* and the *Voice of the Negro*.[17]

Racial uplift and protest poems include "Crispus Attucks," "A Hero of San Juan [Hill]," and "Honor's Appeal to Justice." The first two exhibit a black literary response to nationalism and are reminiscent of Paul Laurence Dunbar's "Black Samson of Brandywine" and Phillis Wheatley's "To His Excellency General Washington." Furthermore, "A Hero of San Juan [Hill]" implies the influence of Boston's integrationist atmosphere. Bush-Banks transforms her praise for the black troops in the Spanish-American War into a call for activism:

> March on, dark sons of Afric's race,
>   Naught can be gained by standing still;
> Retreat not, 'quit yourselves like men,
>   And, like these heroes, climb the hill.
>
> Till pride and prejudice shall cease;
>   Till racial barriers are unknown.

Attain the heights where over all,
Equality shall sit enthroned.

"Honor's Appeal to Justice" is even more explicit. Through twelve stanzas of iambic tetrameter, Bush-Banks condemns racial stereotypes and damns the assertion that black Americans are innately criminal:

Unjust, untrue, is he who dares
Upon our honor to intrude,
And claims that with the sin of crime
The Negro's nature is imbued.

Shall we keep silent? No; thrice No!
We stand defenceless in our cause.
If voices fail to cry aloud
And plead a right to justice's laws.

"At Harvest Time" and "The Walk to Emmaus" recall the Fireside Poets' hymn poems, full of the metaphors of revivalism—Jesus the Redeemer, Salvation, and Heaven. They also show what Benjamin E. Mays has noted concerning the traditional African-American perspective: that "God is the ideal toward which the race struggles . . . He gives the Negro friends." [18]

*Original Poems* is a self-conscious first effort. Almost without exception, the poems conform to the literary conventions of their era. But the race-pride works give the volume historical merit, and as such the collection provides valuable insight into one "colored" woman's integrationist thought at the turn of the century. The collection also mirrors the passing of pastoral values during America's postbellum ground swell toward literary realism. By 1914, Bush-Banks was lifted by this tide as well.

Bush-Banks cites the inspiration for her next volume, *Driftwood:*

Each morning as I watched little Italian children gathering bits of driftwood for the evening fire, vying with each other in childish delight, I fancied what a joyous sight it would be as they sat around the evening fire, and I imagined that the firelight streaming through the windows would brighten up the way of some weary homeward traveler.

In the evening, from out the upper window of my Uncle's little cabin [in Newport, Rhode Island], I looked across the bay to New London [Connecticut], from whose harbor those palatial New York steamers sailed forth upon their mighty voyages. I thought, perhaps these may never return to their safe harbor, and yet, some shattered wreck might give warmth for an evening fire. Perhaps in our lives the driftwood of experience might enable some fellow traveler from afar to catch a gleam of courage and serve the purpose of a guiding hand.

I have also a vivid memory of Newport harbor at the end of a summer day, in the crimson glow of a setting sun.

I have not meant to stray from my theme of fellowship, indeed I could not, because so often rare friendships have inspired me to retain in verse their precious memories, distant in kind, yet near in human understanding.[19]

Superior to *Original Poems* in theme and organization, *Driftwood* has been described by William H. Robinson as "an ambitious failure that succeeds."[20] It consists of nine divisions based on an ocean motif: "Driftwood" (a trilogy); "Bits;" "The Tide Surges"; "Lights Along Shore"; "The Moaning of the Tide"; "The Brightening of the Hearth-Side"; "The Burning Logs of Memory"; "Dreams by the Driftwood Fire"; and "A Floating Spar." Twenty-five poems and two prose pieces fall roughly into the categories of ode, elegy, nature/religious, personal, race pride, and protest. Moreover, several works are reprinted from *Original Poems*, and remarks by Ella Wheeler Wilcox and Paul Laurence Dunbar appear under *Driftwood*'s "Comments."

The "Driftwood" trilogy, consisting of "Morning," "Evening," and "Drifting," underscores Bush-Banks's technical and imaginative expertise. Using iambic pentameter, she makes each poem serve as a distinct chronological and philosophical stage in her perception of reality. "Morning" sets the wood-gathering scene. "Evening" brings the storm with its metaphor of wrecks, both wooden and human. "Drifting" concludes with the imagery of a brilliant sunset at Newport, Rhode Island. Bush-Banks shows she accepts both life and death, anticipating being "Full safely moored within Heaven's harbor bright."

The trilogy technique was standard in nineteenth-century didactic poetry, as evinced in Whittier's "Burning Driftwood" and Longfellow's "Tales of a Wayside Inn." Dunbar's probable response to Bush-Banks's "Driftwood" is his poem "To Pfrimmer (Lines on reading 'Driftwood')." His query to the author, "Did this wood come floating thick/ All along down 'Injin Crick'?" may well refer to Bush-Banks's mixed-blood descent.[21]

Works such as "Abraham Lincoln," "Frederic[k] Douglass," and "To the Memory of Paul La[u]rence Dunbar" exemplify the lyric tradition in *Driftwood*. In particular, the elegy on Dunbar favors Wheatley's "On the Death of the Rev. Mr. George Whitfield." Bush-Banks uses neoclassic language, enjambment, and an effective conclusion to produce a polished, moving tribute.

Her odes go beyond simple commemoration by injecting connotations of current affairs. An example is "Unchained (1863)," where Bush-Banks first celebrates freedom, then criticizes Reconstruction's failure to enforce civil rights, and then demands an end to racial violence. A more traditional

salutation is the ballad "Carney, The Brave Standard Bearer."
At the battle of Fort Wagner, Sergeant William H. Carney
of the all-black 54th Massachusetts regiment sustained serious wounds yet upheld the Union flag. This incident, along
with an ensuing furor over retroactive pay for the 54th, added
to the patriotic variety of racial uplift poetry.[22]

The issues of racism and equality are also found in "Heart-
Throbs" and "The Nation's Evil." While the former decries
discrimination in melancholic, understated tones, "The Nation's Evil" graphically portrays lynch law; Bush-Banks vis-
ualizes "a fierce, blood-thirsty mob," eager to "Add torture
to a quivering frame." Here one finds echoes of James M.
Whitfield's "America" and W. E. B. Du Bois' "Jesus Christ
in Texas."

Although *Driftwood* does not abandon the serene optimism
of family and nature poems, it clearly illustrates Bush-Banks's
growing emphasis on realism. The volume concludes with
"Hope," an essay and free-verse poem in which she contends
that, in spite of disfranchisement in the South and the "volcanic fires of prejudice in the North," the "floating spar of
Hope is seen, making its way toward Right and Justice."
Bush-Banks calls for black leaders who will not only promote
education but will publicize injustices as well. While *Driftwood* embraces the nineteenth-century concept of individual
moral regeneration to eradicate social evils, it also includes
the race-pride and self-help philosophies highlighting African-American thought in the Progressive Era.

Bush-Banks's one-act play, *Memories of Calvary: An Easter
Sketch* (c. 1917), is an example of the late nineteenth-century
"Sunday school" play. Its preface deprecates the "many doctrines of the present day" and "the rapid advance of materialism" that sap man's spiritual strength and peace. The evan-
gelistic reform movement sweeping early twentieth-century

America is suggested in Bush-Banks's exaltation of Christ as "the Highest Ideal." In the first scene, the "Anxious Seeker" is guided by "Night," who soliloquizes on temporal distractions. Resurrection morning dawns just before the beginning of Scene II, and the play ends with the Anxious Seeker "witnessing" Christ and with the singing of hymns. Bush-Banks wrote several plays in the same vein, but *Memories of Calvary* is her only published example.

Bush-Banks left numerous unpublished poems, plays, sketches, and essays, totaling approximately sixty items. They parallel the genres found in her published works and were composed mainly after 1920. In these later writings, she made less use of neoclassic devices, but in some of them she retained her didactic and Native American sensibilities. She also employed more free verse and included elements of negritude, satire, exoticism, and socialism.

Fragments of the play *Indian Trails; or, Trail of the Montauk* form a particularly intriguing element in Bush-Banks's Native American expression. This play was performed at Booker T. Washington High School in Norfolk, Virginia, sometime between 1919 and 1929 while Bush-Banks made a literary tour of the Southeast. In her memoirs, *The Lure of the Distances,* she declares that the philanthropist Maggie Walker patronized the play and urged others to do likewise:

> My visit to Richmond, VA, was memorable indeed because of the hospitable attitude of that magnificent distinguished woman Maggie Walker, founder of a notable business enterprise offering employment to many capable women of all ages. Mme Walker was deeply interested in my dramatic programs of Indian life, and she followed up this interest by introducing me to an audience of more than 2,000 people, urging them to become patrons of my Play—*The Trail of the Montauk.* . . .

From Richmond, I visited Norfolk where I was graciously received by Prof. Jaycox, Principal of Booker Washington High School, and given the privilege of presenting my Indian Play . . . with a cast of . . . beautiful girls, who were obviously pleased to cooperate with me. Our play was a real success, financially and otherwise. It assisted in replenishing the School Library.[23]

*Indian Trails* was probably written as a defensive response to the 1910 *Benson* decision mentioned earlier. An overview of character names shows correspondences to languages that were mutually intelligible from eastern Long Island to the Connecticut–Rhode Island shore lines.[24] For example, Wan-to-co-no-mese ("Montauk's Wise Man") resembles the Narragansett term *Wautaconemese*, "an English youth." Natick expressions for "wise" are *waantam*, "he is wise," *waantash*, "be thou wise," and *wantamoonk*, "wisdom, being wise."[25] The names and functions of the characters Quashawan ("Montauk's Wise Woman") and Sequanah ("Maker of bowls and backboards") are rooted in Algonquian social custom and material culture. Names like Dawn-of-Day and Fleet-of-Foot characterize the abundance of nouns present in the vocabularies of the last known Montauk speakers.

Bush-Banks's most significant unpublished works are the series entitled *Aunt Viney's Sketches* (c. 1920–1932), which feature a black female folk character based on a composite of Harlem residents. Bush-Banks completed twelve skits by 1932. Of the surviving seven, five have recently been published.[26] Each of the sketches presents Aunt Viney in different humorous adventures, which she manages to transpose into commentaries on African-American politics, culture, religion, and so on. "Miss Ollie," the white proprietress of a Harlem gift shop, is Aunt Viney's sounding board.

*Aunt Viney's Sketches* are important for several reasons. Aunt

Viney precedes the appearance of Langston Hughes's "Jesse
B. Simple" character by at least six years. In contrast to nearly
all other black dialect characters, Aunt Viney is an assertive,
positive figure. And as a female folk character, she upholds
the validity of traditional (black) values in an urban world.

In addition to producing the *Aunt Viney* series, Bush-Banks
explored the primitivist spirit of the Negro Renaissance. Her
dramatic monologue "Shadows: Dedicated to Miss Marian
Anderson" celebrates the African heritage. It features a prologue, a free-verse poem, and accompanying interpretive
dancing. Its central figure is "Nolanda, the African maiden,"
who dances in the "pitiless white light of advanced civilization." This white light casts "shadows" on African peoples.
Bush-Banks turns the somber shades into an affirmative statement—the darkness is actually "SHADOWS from the realm
of rich African attainment." Like Claude McKay's "The
Harlem Dancer" and Hughes's "Dream Variations," "Shadows" evokes the cult of native purity underlying negritude.
In a similar vein are Bush-Banks's poems "Barthe (a brown
sculptor, after viewing the bust of his 'Tortured Negro')"
and "Harlem."

Bush-Banks solves a contemporary problem with an old
but effective solution in the vignette called "Black Communism." The protagonist is Wyatt Hendricks, who rejects the
violence associated with communism in favor of a more
peaceful Christian socialist approach. Bush-Banks uses this
character to distinguish between acceptable and unacceptable
actions in the battle against avarice. The vignette parallels
her unpublished poem "The Keepers of the House (in memory of Eugene Debs)," which reveals a marked political un-
dercurrent, but in its depiction of Wyatt's compassionate dis-
tribution of food and the thankfulness he inspires among its
recipients, the story also continues the use of Christian imagery found throughout her works.

It is not known if Bush-Banks voted for or formally joined socialist-oriented groups, but her sympathies are obvious. As in numerous other works, "Black Communism" stresses her ongoing concern with what she perceived was the twentieth century's spiritual malaise. Her message is clear: People of color can effect change within the system *and* escape suspicion about their patriotism if they practice a sort of updated nineteenth-century liberalism, incorporating self-reliance, benevolence, and humanitarianism.

Ultimately Bush-Banks comes full circle in her unpublished writings by adapting nineteenth-century values to twentieth-century technological and moral issues. And even though the appeal of Native American topics dwindled in the new age, Bush-Banks held fast to her dual inheritance. One is left with the image of a woman who adjusted to both eras, but who preferred the spirituality of yesteryear to the materialism of modern life.[27]

## NOTES

1. Autobiographical ms., opposite front, in Olivia Ward Bush [-Banks], *Driftwood* (Cranston, RI: Atlantic Printing Co., 1914), Harris Collection of American Poetry and Plays, John Hay Library, Brown University, Providence, RI. This manuscript has been reproduced in the Appendix at the end of this volume.

2. Autobiographical cryptic notation ms., in the Olivia Ward Bush-Banks Papers, Amistad Research Center, Tulane University, New Orleans, LA. This notation, along with another brief note (cf. n. 12), possibly form part of the missing first chapter of Bush-Banks's unpublished memoirs, *The Lure of the Distances*, which are included in this volume.

3. Autobiographical ms.

4. Letter to Ella Wheeler Wilcox, in Wilcox, "Is She the Reincarnation of Queen Cleopatra?" *Boston American* (20 Oct. 1912), n. p., Bush-Banks Papers. See also the Appendix in this volume.

5. Autobiographical ms. Photographs of Bush-Banks in conventional and tribal dress are in the possession of the editor.

6. See *The History and Archaeology of the Montauk Indians*, Suffolk County Archaeological Association, Readings in Long Island Archaeology and Ethnohistory 3 (Lexington, MA: Ginn, 1979).

7. Extensive genealogical information on the Poosepatuck and Shinnecock native groups is contained in the Ader E. Martin Indian Scrapbooks (Harry B. Squires, comp.), Suffolk County Historical Society, Riverhead, NY. A special thanks is extended to Miss Dorothy T. King, Librarian of the Long Island Collection at the East Hampton Free Library, East Hampton, NY, Mr. Daniel Kaplan, Assistant Curator of the Library of Anthropology at the Nassau County Museum, Sands Point Preserve, Port Washington, NY, and Mrs. Kathleen Tucker of Sag Harbor, NY for their assistance in locating data on the Poosepatuck and Montauk Indian tribes.

8. Donald Treadwell, personal interview, Poosepatuck Indian Reservation, 27 July 1984; Michael and Peggy Cause, personal interviews, Shinnecock Indian Reservation, 28 July 1987; Asiba Tupahache (Matinecoc Longhouse of Long Island, Inc.), personal interview, 28 July 1987.

9. *Annual Report of the Montauk Tribe of Indians for the Year 1916* (n.p., n.d.), pp. 7, 12–13. Nassau County Museum, Sands Point Preserve Anthropological Library, Port Washington, NY.

10. John Daniels, *In Freedom's Birthplace: A Study of the Boston Negroes* (1914; rpt. New York: Negro University Press, 1968), p. 212.

11. Autobiographical cryptic notation ms., Bush-Banks Papers.

12. Second autobiographical notation, ts., Bush-Banks Papers. The Abyssinia Community Center was a part of Adam Clayton Powell, Sr.'s Abyssinia Baptist Church in Harlem.

13. Richmond Barthe, personal interview, 11 Oct. 1981; Elizabeth Bowser, personal interview, 24 Feb. 1988.

14. Carter G. Woodson, letter to Olivia Ward Bush-Banks, 22 Dec. 1938, Bush-Banks Papers. See also the Appendix in this volume.

15. Esther Washington Smith, personal interview, 15 Sept. 1974;

and Helen Horton, personal interview, 10 Oct. 1981; I am in-
debted to Miss Horton for giving me my initial access to the Bush-
Banks Papers. Other family informants include Nathalie Lockhart
Forrest; Rose Marie Roby; and Alfreida A. Lockhart Figueroa. See
also Olivia Ward Bush-Banks, *The Lure of the Distances.*

16. John Greenleaf Whittier, "The Poetry of Heart and Home,"
*National Era* (9 Sept. 1847), quoted in Lewis Leary, *John Green-
leaf Whittier,* United States Authors Series, vol. 6 (New York:
Twayne, 1961), p. 88; and William Cullen Bryant, *The Lectures on
Poetry* (1825–1826), quoted in Albert F. McLean, Jr., *William
Cullen Bryant,* United States Authors Series, vol. 68 (New York:
Twayne, 1964), pp. 109–11.

17. "Voices" appeared in *Voice of the Negro* 2, no. 2 (1905):
400.

18. Benjamin E. Mays, *The Negro's God as Reflected in His Literature* (1938; rpt. New York: Atheneum, 1968), pp. 130–31.

19. Notation on origin of *Driftwood* theme, ms., Bush-Banks
Papers.

20. William H. Robinson, *Black New England Letters: The Uses
of Writings in Black New England,* NEH Learning Library Program, no. 2 (Boston, MA: Boston Public Library, 1977), p. 124.
See also Ann Allen Shockley, *Afro-American Women Writers 1746–
1933: A Critical Anthology and Guide* (New York: G. K. Hall,
1988), pp. 292, 341–45.

21. *The Complete Poems of Paul Laurence Dunbar* (New York:
Dodd, Mead and Co., 1929), p. 277.

22. Bush-Banks may have known Carney personally. He resided
in Boston from the end of the Civil War until his death in 1908.

23. From Ch. 3, "The Gleam and the Glow: Southern Hospitality," in *The Lure of the Distances.* Maggie L. Walker established
the Richmond (Virginia) Consolidated Bank and Trust Company
and supported a variety of philanthropic organizations, such as a
tuberculosis sanitorium, a training center for girls, and a community center.

24. Bernice F. Guillaume, "Character Names in *Indian Trails*
by Olivia Ward Bush (Banks): Clues to Afro Assimilation into Long

Island's Native Americans." *Afro-Americans in New York Life and History* 10, no. 2 (1986): 45–53.

25. James H. Trumball, *Natick Dictionary,* Smithsonian Institution, Bureau of American Ethnology, *Bulletin* 25 (Washington, D.C.: Government Printing Office, 1903), p. 245; cited in Guillaume, p. 47.

26. Bernice F. Guillaume, "The Female as Harlem Sage: The 'Aunt Viney's Sketches' of Olivia Ward Bush-Banks," *Langston Hughes Review* 6, no. 2 (1987): 1–10. See also the Appendix in this volume, "Letter from Olivia Ward Bush-Banks to N. R. Stantley."

27. Gratitude is extended to Drs. R. Baxter Miller and John Hope Franklin for advice leading to the creation of this volume.

# EDITORIAL NOTE

Unless specified, Bush-Banks's unpublished works are contained in her personal papers at the Amistad Research Center, Tulane University, New Orleans. The reader will note that minor changes in spelling and punctuation are occasionally inserted in brackets for the sake of textual clarity and continuity. Otherwise her works, both published and unpublished are presented as Bush-Banks wrote them.

Finally, every effort has been made to provide a comprehensive scope of the author's works. Any errors or omissions are the sole responsibility of the editor.

# PUBLISHED WORKS: POEMS
## *1899–1916*

❧ ❧ ❧

This Little Booklet
Is DEDICATED WITH
PROFOUND REVERENCE AND RESPECT
TO THE PEOPLE OF MY RACE,
The Afro-Americans,
BY
MRS. OLIVIA BUSH,
OF
PROVIDENCE, R. I.


"Judge us not, O favored races,
　　From the heights we have attained;
Rather measure our progression
　　By the depths from whence we came."

# ORIGINAL POEMS

## MORNING ON SHINNECOCK

The rising sun had crowned the hills,
 And added beauty to the plain;
O grand and wondrous spectacle!
 That only nature could explain.

I stood within a leafy grove,
 And gazed around in blissful awe;
The sky appeared one mass of blue,
 That seemed to spread from sea to shore.

Far as the human eye could see,
 Were stretched the fields of waving corn.
Soft on my ear the warbling birds
 Were herding the birth of morn.

While here and there a cottage quaint
 Seemed to repose in quiet ease
Amid the trees, whose leaflets waved
 And fluttered in the passing breeze.

O morning hour! so dear thy joy,
 And how I longed for thee to last;
But e'en thy fading into day
 Brought me an echo of the past.

This collection was originally published in Providence, RI, by the Press of Louis A. Basinet, 1899. Reproduced in this volume by courtesy of the Harris Collection of American Poetry and Plays, John Hay Library, University, Providence, RI.

'Twas this,—how fair my life began;
　　How pleasant was its hour of dawn;
But, merging into sorrow's day,
　　Then beauty faded with the morn.


## TREASURED MOMENTS

For a time away from the tumult,
　　Shut in from the care and the strife,
Away from the gloom and the discord,
　　That seemed to encircle my life.

Shut in with the dear, earnest women—
　　Women with hearts true and strong,
Who dared to face a great evil,
　　Who dared to contend against wrong.

And the speaker's words were so cheering,
　　As she talked to us of the time
When the women crusaded together;
　　How they battled against the wine.

How they fought against deadly poison;
　　How they struggled again and again,
Till some homes were made better and brighter,
　　Till some hearts were robbed of their pain.

Then the speaker's tones grew more tender,
　　As she spoke of a life so complete,
That many lives caught the essence
　　Of her life so full and so sweet;

Who had just stepped over the threshold,
　　And had entered the "Great Beyond,"
Life's labor so nobly completed,
　　Heaven's blessing triumphantly won.

Then sweet rose the voice of the singer,
Singing of "Christ and the Cross,"
Till my soul cried loudly within me
"I'll count everything but as dross."

For His sake who bore our great burden,
Who labored and suffered so long;
And my heart grew glad for the singer,
And I said: "O praise God for the song!"

Ah! how I was strengthened, uplifted.
How the depths of my soul were stirred;
And the words, the song and the music
Seemed the sweetest I ever had heard.

I thought when that hour was ended,
I shall cherish its memory so long;
I shall think of the words so inspiring.
I shall think of the singer, the song.

As I wended my way again homeward,
Possessed with a sweet, nameless peace,
I thought of the great Life Eternal
Where such moments as these never cease.

Where there's fullness of joy forever,
Where we meet an unbroken band,
Shut in with the dear, blessed Master;
Resting safe at the Father's right hand.

## AT HARVEST TIME

A Sower walked among his fields
When Spring's fair glory filled the earth;
He scattered seed with eager hand,
And sowing, thought upon their worth.

"These seeds are precious ones," he said.
    "The finest flowers shall be mine;
And I shall reap rich, golden grain,
    When these are ripe at harvest time."

"I'll watch their growth with earnest care,
    And faithfully will till the soil;
With willing hands each passing day
    From morn till setting sun I'll toil.
And when the reaping time shall come,
    A bounteous Harvest shall be mine;
I shall rejoice at duty done
    When these are ripe at Harvest time."

Forth to his fields at Harvest time,
    The Sower bent his steps again;
The Reapers' song sang merrily,
    Their sickles gleamed 'mid golden grain.
With joyous heart the Sower cried
    "Behold, what precious sheaves are mine;
And labor brings its own reward,
    For these are ripe at Harvest time."

O Master! in thy fields so fair
    We, too, are sowing precious seed.
And like the Sower we will toil
    Till golden grain fulfil thy need.
Then shall we hear thy loving voice,—
    "Behold! what precious sheaves are mine.
Let all be safely garnered in,
    For these are ripe at Harvest time."

## A HERO OF SAN JUAN [HILL]

Among the sick and wounded ones,
    This stricken soldier boy lay,

With glassy eye and shortened breath;
   His life seemed slipping fast away.

My heart grew faint to see him thus,
   His dark brown face so full of pain,
I wondered if the mother's eyes
   Were looking for her boy in vain.

I bent to catch his feeble's words:
   "I am so ill and far from home.
I feel so strange and lonely here;
   You seem a friend, I'm glad you've come.

"I want to tell you how our boys
   Went charging on the enemy.
'Twas when we climbed up Juan's hill;
   And there we got the victory.

"The Spaniards poured a heavy fire;
   We met it with a right good will.
We saw the Seventy-first fall back,
   And then our boys went up the hill.

"Yes, up the hill, and gained it, too;
   Not one brave boy was seen to lag.
Old Glory o'er us floating free,
   We'd gladly died for that old flag."

His dim eye brightened as he spoke;
   He seemed unconscious of his pain;
In fancy on the battlefield
   He lived that victory o'er again.

And I; I seemed to grasp it, too,—
   The stalwart from, the dusky face
Of those black heroes, climbing up
   To win fair glory for their race.

The Spaniards said that phalanx seemed
  To move like one black, solid wall;
They flung defiance back at Death,
  And, answering to that thrilling call,

They fought for Cuban liberty.
  On Juan's hill those bloody stains
Mark how these heroes won the day
  And added honor to their names.

March on, dark sons of Afric's race,
  Naught can be gained by standing still;
Retreat not, 'quit yourselves like men,
  And, like these heroes, climb the hill,

Till pride and prejudice shall cease;
  Till racial barriers are unknown.
Attain the heights where over all,
  Equality shall sit enthroned.


## CRISPUS ATTUCKS

The Nation's heart beat wildly,
  And keenly felt the coming strife;
The Country's call was sounding
  Brave men must offer life for life.

So long Great Britain's power
  Had sternly held unyielding sway,
The people yearned for freedom
  And cried, "Our blood must pave the way."

So, on the streets of Boston,
  Where madly rushed the British foe;

Men questioned with each other,
   "Who shall be first to strike the blow?"

Not that they shrank from duty,
   Ah, no! their lives they gladly gave;
But War, with all its terrors,
   Brings fear to hearts both true and brave.

But one, with fearless courage,
   Inspired them to activity,
And boldly led them forward
   With cheering shout, "For Liberty?"

In face of death and danger,
   He met the foe, this soldier true,
Till, charging full upon them,
   Their bayonets had pierced him through.

He fell, and o'er the pavement
   A Negro's blood was flowing free.
His sable hand was foremost
   To strike the blow for liberty.

It was a deed most valiant,
   And mighty was the work begun,
For War then waging fiercely,
   Ceased not till victory was won.

Naught but a slave was Attucks,
   And yet how grand a hero, too.
He gave a life for freedom,
   What more could royal sovereign do?

Well may we eulogize him!
   And rear a monument of fame.
We hold his memory sacred;
   We honor and revere his name.

A century has vanished,
    Yet, through the years still rolling on
We emulate his bravery
    And praise the deed he nobly done.

Then write in glowing letters
    These thrilling words in history,—
That Attucks was a hero,
    That Attucks died for Liberty.


# HONOR'S APPEAL TO JUSTICE

Unjust, untrue, is he who dares
    Upon our honor to intrude,
And claims that with the sin of crime
    The Negro's nature is imbued.

Shall we keep silent? No; thrice No!
    We stand defenceless in our cause.
If voices fail to cry aloud
    And plead a right to justice's laws.

For who shall vindicate this wrong?
    Who shall defend our perjured race?
We must speak out with one accord,
    If we the stigma would erase.

The cruel hand that raised the lash
    To strike a wronged and helpless race,
Is stained with sin of deepest dye,
    And shows of brutal crime more trace.

I draw a picture of the slave
    Who meekly bowed 'neath stinging blows

And raised no hand in swift defense,
    To kill, to threaten, or oppose.

I hear from out his cabin rise
    Sweet songs of praises unto God.
E'en with his painful wounds he sings,
    And utters no resentful word.

I see him in the darker days
    When blood like crimson rivers ran,
And Southern slavers left their homes
    In answer to stern war's demands.

They left their lands, their kindred ties,
    Entrusted to the Slave alone.
Who faithfully and nobly strove
    To guard the sacred rights of home.

Yes; even lives were in his hands.
    Yet he, though held in slavery,
Upon his honor threw no shame,
    Or stain of criminality.

Today, on equal ground he stands
    With loyal, true, and noble men.
He loves his country, and remains
    A law abiding citizen.

He shares no part in daring plot,
    He scorns to hint of anarchy;
He only asks his native right;
    Can this be criminality?

Then, Justice! we implore thy aid.
    Thine arm can well supply our need;
Protect our name, assist our cause,
    For Right and Right alone we plead.

# THE WALK TO EMMAUS

'Twas eventide. Along the dusty road
   Two weary travelers passed with aching feet
And heavy hearts, while each in saddened tones
   The story of their Lord would oft repeat.

We yearn for Him, and is it not three days
   Since first He lay within the silent tomb?
Yet when we hastened to His resting place,
   Our Lord had gone; His grave was wrapt in gloom.

Communing thus, these weary travelers went.
   Their hearts oppressed by mingled doubt and fear;
When lo! along the road to Emmaus
   Their Lord, the risen Christ Himself, drew near.

With gentle voice He asked of them their grief,—
   "Why are ye sad? and O, what troubleth thee?"
They knew not that the loving Master spoke,
   Their eyes were holden, that they could not see.

And one replied: "We know not where He is,—
   Our Lord, who promised Israel to redeem.
Art thou a stranger in Jerusalem?
   And knowest not what marvelous things have been?"

Then Jesus spoke. "Why are ye show of heart?
   Did not the prophets in the days of old
Proclaim that Christ must die and live again,
   That ye His wondrous power might behold?"

Their hearts were touched; the Master's thrilling words
   Dispelled their fears and cleared their darkened sight.
And while the Holy Scriptures He declared,
   There came sweet peace and filled their souls with light.

The Master ceased, and now the journey o'er
  He still would further go along the road.
But they constrained Him, saying: "Tarry here;
  Abide with us and enter our abode."

He deigned to pass within that humble home,
  His holy presence filled the place with light;
He sat at meat and brake and blessed the bread,
  And ere they know it vanished from their sight.

They said, with gladdened hearts, "It is our Lord,
  Our risen Christ for whom we long have yearned;
We knew Him not when walking by the way,
  And yet our hearts within us sweetly burned.

O Christian! walking o'er Life's rugged road,
  Thou too, like His disciples, oft shall say,—
"Did not our hearts within us sweetly burn
  When Jesus talked with us beside the way?"


## MY DREAM OF THE NEW YEAR

Through the waning hours of moments
  Of the slowly dying year,
I sat watching, watching, waiting
  For the New Dawn to appear.
While the Old Year's strife and struggle,
  With its changing, varied scene,
Passed before me till I wearied,
  Fell asleep—asleep to dream

That I saw a lofty Castle,
  Vast in size and wondrous fair;

And I stood outside its portal
  Knocking for an entrance there.
From its towers the bells were ringing
  In a strange, discordant tone,
Wailing out their mournful measures
  Like a mortal's dying moan.

Still I waited, knocked and waited,
  For I longed to enter there;
Longed to know the name and secret
  Of this Castle, vast and fair.
When a voice within cried loudly,
  "Thou shalt have that wish of thine.
Thou art knocking at Life's Castle,
  And the keeper's name is Time.

"And the bells you hear above you
  Ring out all the dying years;
Ring out Man's past griefs and sorrows,
  Ring out blasted hopes and fears.
With the coming of the New Year
  They will cease that refrain.
You will hear them chiming sweetly,
  Ringing out a joyous strain.

"If you watch and wait with patience,
  You shall be admitted here;
For the New Year swift approaches,
  Its bright dawning draweth near."
So I waited, watched and waited
  Till the Castle's door swung wide;
And the keeper bade me enter,
  Saying, "Mortal here abide."

'Twas indeed a wondrous Castle,
  With its arches gleaming bright,

E'en the keeper's face was beaming
   With a rare and radiant light.
Through its spacious halls he led me
   Over floors of spotless white,
Till it seemed that mortal vision
   Ne'er beheld a fairer sight.

On its walls in blazoned letters
   I could trace each written word,
Words that could not fail to strengthen
   When by mortals they were heard.
And the keeper, softly speaking,
   Read them, one by one, to me,—
"Resolution, faith, and duty,
   Hope and opportunity."

Then I asked him, "Can you tell me
   Why these words are written here?"
He replied: "These are the watchwords
   That shall guide thee through the year.
Just resolve to do thy duty;
   Thine the opportunity.
Hope shall aid thee in thy purpose,
   Do it well and faithfully."

Then the bells pealed out so loudly,
   Ringing out their joyous strain,
That I started from my slumber,
   Found myself alone again.
Saw no more Life's wondrous Castle,
   Vanished now the keeper Time;
Heard no more the joyful pealing
   Of the bells' sweet, tuneful chime.

Day had dawned, the night was over,
   Life's Old year was safely past.

Now had dawned a brighter morning,
Life's New Year had come at last.
But the Dream had filled its mission—
Made my path of duty clear.
Hope and Faith were now the watchwords
Brightening up my glad New Year.

## DRIFTING

And now the sun in tinted splendor sank,
The west was all aglow with crimson light;
The bay seemed like a sheet of burnished gold,
Its waters glistened with such radiance bright.

At anchor lay the yachts with snow-white sails,
Outlined against glowing, rose-hued sky.
No ripple stirred the waters' calm repose
Save when a tiny craft sped lightly by.

Our boat was drifting slowly, gently round,
To rest secure till evening shadows fell;
No sound disturbed the stillness of the air,
Save the soft chiming of the vesper bell.

Yes, drifting, drifting; and I thought that life,
When nearing death, is like the sunset sky.
And death is but the slow, sure drifting in
To rest far more securely, by and by.

Then let me drift along the Bay of Time,
Till my last sun shall set in glowing light;
Let me cast anchor where no shadows fall,
Forever moored within Heaven's harbor bright.

Newport, June 12, 1898.

# VOICES

I stand upon the haunted plain
    Of vanished day and year,
And ever o'er its gloomy waste
    Some strange, sad voice I hear.
Some voice from out the shadowed Past;
    And one I call Regret,
And one I know is Misspent Hours,
    Whose memory lingers yet.

Then Failure speaks in bitter tones,
    And Grief, with all its woes;
Remorse, whose deep and cruel stings
    My painful thoughts disclose.
Thus do these voices speak to me,
    And flit like shadows past;
My spirit falters in despair,
    And tears flow thick and fast.

But when, within the wide domain
    Of Future Day and Year
I stand, and o'er its sunlit Plain
    A sweeter Voice I hear,
Which bids me leave the darkened Past
    And crush its memory,—
I'll listen gladly, and obey
    The Voice of Opportunity.

# A PICTURE

I drew a picture long ago—
 A picture of a sullen sea;
A picture that I value now
 Because it clears Life's mystery.

My sea was dark and full of gloom;
 I painted rocks of sombre hue.
My sky alone bespoke of light,
 And that I painted palest blue.

But e'en across my sky of blue
 Stretched troubled clouds of sodden gray,
Through which the sun shone weak and dim,
 With only here and there a ray.

Around my rocks the yellow foam
 Seemed surging, moaning in despair
As if the waves, their fury spent,
 Left naught but desolation there.

Three crafts with fluttering sails I drew,
 And one sailed near the rocks of gray,
The other on its westward course,
 Went speeding out of danger's way.

The other still outdistanced them
 Where sky and water seemed to met.

Credit is due to Ann Allen Shockley for discovering this poem in the *Colored American Magazine* 1 (June 1900): 77–78.

I painted that with sails full set,
    And then my picture was complete.

My life was like the sullen sea,
    Misfortunes, woes, my rocks of gray,
The crafts portrayed Life's changing scenes,
    The clouded sky Life's troubled Day.

I longed to paint that picture o'er
    Without the rocks of sombre hue;
Without the troubled clouds of gray,
    I'll paint the sky of brightest blue.

My sea shall lay in calm repose,
    No hint of surging, moaning sigh.
My crafts, unhindered by the rocks,
    Shall speed in joyous swiftness by.

But this shall be when brightest hours
    Of hope and cheer are given me.
I'll paint this picture when Life's sun
    Shines clear upon Prosperity.

*Yours sincerely*

*Olivia Ward Bush*

# Driftwood

— BY —

## OLIVIA WARD BUSH

## To the Sacred Memory

of

My Aunt,

## Maria Draper,

Who loved me unceasingly, labored untiringly,
Sacrificing willingly for me her own life's
interests this little book

is

Most affectionately dedicated.

# CONTENTS

———

# COMMENTS

I like your book very much, especially the poem Drifting. There is a high spiritual tone about it that is bound to please. "Voices" pleases me also.

Your book should be an inspiration to the women of our race, do not hesitate to quote whatever you may wish from what I say.

Sincerely yours,<br>PAUL LAURENCE DUNBAR.

July, 1904.

The lines in the poem, "A Tribute to Paul Laurence Dunbar," have much merit in them. I think your command of English in prose is quite remarkable.

Sincerely yours,<br>ELLA WHEELER WILCOX.

# INTRODUCTION

I have stood on the shore, and watched the waters surging land-ward, then receding ever in alternate motion. I have seen driftwood strewn along the sand, cast up by the restless waves.

I have heard the merry shouts of children, as they gathered, one by one, bits, for the driftwood fire which has warmed and cheered the lowly dwellings, scattered along shore, or perchance its gleaming blaze shining far out into the night has led some lone traveller to his home.

I have thought how oft these bits of driftwood are but the poor misshapen remnant of some bark wrecked on its homeward course and still the drift-wood fire burns bright and still its warmth and glow cheers up Earth's dreary places.

These verses are but bits of driftwood cast up by the landward-surging and receding waters of adversity and prosperity, and the author has gathered them with the fond hope that some light shall gleam from these pages far out into the night of human perplex-ities, and brighten up the homeward way of some discouraged traveller.

OLIVIA WARD BUSH.

# Driftwood

Sung by the strand to the music of the wave.

———————

## MORNING

Bright glows the morn, I pace the shining sands,
And watch the children, as with eager hands
They gather driftwood for the evening fire.
Their merry laughter, ringing loud and clear,
Resounds like sweetest music to my ear,
As swift they toil, each with the same desire.

And now their task completed, they depart,
Each one with beaming face and happy heart,
They too, will watch the driftwood fire to-night,
And knowing this, they hasten glad and gay,
With willing feet, along the homeward way,
Their precious burdens bearing with delight.

I watch these little children of the poor,
Till they have reached each lowly dwelling's door,
And then, I too my footsteps homeward turn;
I fancy what a joyous sight 'twill be,
To see the children sitting in their glee,
Close by the fire and laugh to see it burn.

### EVENING

From out my open window, I can see
The rolling waves, as fierce and restlessly,
They dash against the long, long stretch of shore,
And in the distance, I can dimly trace,
Some out-bound vessel having left her place
Of Harbor, to return perhaps no more.

Within my mind there dwells this lingering thought,
How oft from ill the greatest good is wrought,
Perhaps some shattered wreck along the strand,
Will help to make the fire burn more bright,
And for some weary traveller to-night,
'Twill serve the purpose of a guiding hand.

Ah yes, and thus it is with these our lives,
Some poor misshapen remnant still survives,
Of what was once a fair and beauteous form,
And yet some dwelling may be made more bright,
Some one afar may catch a gleam of light,
After the fury of the blighting storm.

## Drifting

And now the sun in tinted splendor sank,
  The west was all aglow with crimson light;
The bay seemed like a sheet of burnished gold,
  Its waters glistened with such radiance bright.


At anchor lay the yachts with snow-white sails,
  Outlined against the glowing, rose-hued sky;
No ripple stirred the waters' calm repose
  Save when a tiny craft sped lightly by.


Our boat was drifting slowly, gently round,
  To rest secure till evening shadows fell;
No sound disturbed the stillness of the air,
  Save the soft chiming of the vesper bell.


Yes, drifting, drifting; and I thought that life,
  When nearing death, is like the sunset sky:
And death is but the slow, sure drifting in,
  To rest far more securely, by and by.


Then let me drift along the Bay of time,
  Till my last sun shall set in glowing light;
Let me cast anchor where no shadows fall,
  Full safely moored within Heaven's harbor bright.

  Newport, June 12, 1898.

# Bits

## Fancies

Mid parted clouds, all silver-edged,
   A gleam of fiery gold,
A dash of crimson-varied hues,
   The Sunset Story's told.

A mirrored lake 'tween mossy banks,
   A lofty mountain ridge,
A cottage nestling in the vale
   Seen from a ruined bridge.

A woman longing to discern
   Beyond the gleam of gold
A rush of memory, a sigh,
   And Life's strange tale is told.

## Regret

I said a thoughtless word one day,
A loved one heard and went away;
I cried:"Forgive me, I was blind;
I would not wound or be unkind."
I waited long, but all in vain,
To win my loved one back again.
Too late, alas! to weep and pray,
Death came; my loved one passed away.
Then, what a bitter fate was mine!
No language could my grief define;
Ah! deep regret could not unsay
The thoughtless word I spoke that day.

## At Sunset

I stood in the doorway at evening,
   And I looked to the hills far away
Where the sun's last rays seemed to linger,
   Ere they faded in brilliant display.

Yes, lingered in beautiful splendor,
   And the scene was rare to behold,
A pale blue sky was its back-ground,
   With stretches of pink and gold.

What wonder that Nature's rare beauty
   So inspires the soul and thrills
Our beings with tender emotions,
   As we look far away to the hills!

To the "hills" of which "David" has spoken,
   "From whence comes my help," said he,
And we have the same blest assurance,
   As we gaze on their majesty.

And we think of the Power who formed them,
   They seem like a tower of defence
To protect and to ward off the evil
   Until we depart and go hence;

Where the sunlight fades not, but lingers,
And to-night my waiting soul thrills
As I stand in the doorway at sunset,
As I look far away to the hills.

———————————

## Misjudged

Beneath Misfortune's dark and heavy cloud,
My heart sore wounded, unsubmissive bowed,
Hope after hope within me paled and died,
Until indifference and sullen pride
Usurped my nature's usual warmth and glow
And made Ambition's fire burn dim and low;
And then the world, in worldly wisdom said,
T'were better far that such a life be dead,
Than living thus, so selfish cold and drear,
Ambitionless, devoid of warmth and cheer.
And yet this comfort still remained for me;
The Finite differs from Infinity,
God understands, so I indeed am blest,
He knows it all, and knowing, judges best.

## Overlooked

I turned the pages of my book,
With nervous haste and heedless care,
I searched impatiently to find
Some favorite verses written there.
At last upon the book's first page
I found the lines for which I sought,
But in my haste, had overlooked
And suddenly there came this thought,
How oft for some much-needed thing
We ask the Father o'er and o'er,
When, Lo! by simple faith and trust
We find the blessing at our door.

---

## Inspiration

Within my soul, like flames of living fire,
I feel the burning heat of strong desire
And, speeding like full many an arrow's dart,
Thought after thought swift courses through my
      heart,
I seize my pen with eager fond delight,
Breathe on, sweet Muse of song, that I may write.

## Voices

I stand upon the haunted plain
  Of vanished day and year,
And ever o'er its gloomy waste
  Some strange, sad voice I hear.
Some voice from out the shadowed Past;
  And one I call Regret,
And one I know is Misspent Hours,
  Whose memory lingers yet.

Then Failure speaks in bitter tones,
  And Grief, with all its woes;
Remorse, whose deep and cruel stings
  My painful thoughts disclose.
Thus do these voices speak to me,
  And flit like shadows past;
My spirit falters in despair,
  And tears flow thick and fast.

But when, within the wide domain
  Of Future Day and Year
I stand, and o'er its sunlit Plain
  A sweeter word I hear,
Which bids me leave the darkened Past
  And crush its memory,—
I'll hasten to obey the Voice
  Of Opportunity.

# The Tide Surges

## Heart-Throbs

We suffer and ye know it not,
  Nor yet can ever know,
What depth of bitterness is ours,
  Or why we suffer so;—

If ye would know what anguish is,
  Ask of the dark-skinned race,
Ay! ask of him who lives to know
  The color of his face.

Then plead as he has often pled
  For manhood among men,
And feel the pain of rights denied;
  Thou canst not know till then.

Or share with him for one brief space,
  Ambition's fond desire,
Reach out, and strive, as he has striven,
And aim for something higher.

Let knowledge cultivate, refine,
  Let culture feed the mind,
Then fondly dream of hopes fulfilled,
  And dreaming wake to find;—

That merit worth or patient toil
　　Does not suffice to win.
Then learn the cause of this defeat,
　　The color of the skin.

The mother of the dusky babe,
　　Surveys with aching heart
Bright prospects, knowing all the while,
　　Her off-spring shares no part.

The child attains to manhood's years,
　　Still conscious of the same,
　　While others boast of Life's success,
　　He knows it but in name.

Yes, aim, reach out, aspire and strive
　　And know, "Twere all in vain,
And e'en in Freedom's name appeal,
　　Then ye can sense our pain.

We suffer and ye know it not,
　　Nor yet can ever know,
What depth of bitterness is ours,
　　Or why we suffer so.

# The Nation's Evil

A sound is heard throughout our land,
  A moaning, yearning, pleading cry;
"O mighty Arm of Right stretch forth,
  Crush out our hopeless misery.
I see a weary dark-skinned race
  Bend low beneath Oppression's weight,
I hear their off-spring wailing out,
  O, "Save us from our fathers' fate!"

I see a fierce, blood-thirsty mob,
  Add torture to a quivering frame.
I hear an agonizing cry
  Hushed by the cruel fiery flame.
I see the home left desolate,
  I see a father forced to die,
I hear a mother's anguished groan,
  I hear their children's piteous cry.

How long I ask shall these things be?
  How long shall men have hearts of stone?
My soul grown sick and faint within,
  Cries out in supplicating tone,
"Great God, send forth thy swift demand,
  Declare this evil shall not be,
That man give justice unto man,
  And cease this inhumanity."

[ 67 ]

# Lights Along Shore

## Abraham Lincoln

Like some gigantic, lofty forest tree,
  Shorn of its leafy garment in the storm,
With roots secure deep-fastened in the earth,
  Where naught can rob it of its noble form,
So stood this man, strong in his sense of right,
  Who faltered not, whose courage never failed,
Within the Nation's heart, his image stands
  For aye;—because o'er Wrong he had prevailed.


More than a friend, or brother, then was he,
  In very truth, a Martyr for the Cause,
Unflinching in his zeal-opposing wrong,
  Defending bravely God's own Righteous laws.
For, out of hard almost unyielding rock,
  Did he not hew a passage for our way?
Did he not cause the darkness to disperse,
  Did we not see the dawning of the day?


Live ever in our memories, great soul.
  Tho' passed beyond the pale of human sense,
Thy work well done, hath found its just reward,
  Divine approval is thy recompense.

## Federic Douglass

We would render fitting tribute,
  We would add to thy great fame,
We would crown thee with due honor
  And immortalize thy name.

Till Life's evening closed around thee,
  Thy great love remained the same,
Then from out the Land of Spirits
  Silently the summons came.

In the greatness of thy manhood,
  We can see thee even now,
Stamped upon our hearts thy image,
  Silver hair and noble brow.

"Grand old Statesman," Thou wast loyal
  To thy country and her cause,
By the right of such devotion,
  Thou hast won our just applause.

Orator of noblest order,
  Thine the power to declare,
Thrilling Theme, in tones portraying,
  Eloquence, divinely rare.

Once, in pleading for thy people,
  Who had suffered grevious wrong,
Words like these, intense with feeling
  Fell upon the list'ning throng.


"Judge us not, O! favored races,
  From the lofty heights of fame,
Rather measure our progression,
  By the depths from whence we came.


Telling words, O, Great Defender,
  Of a cause so dear to thee,
Not alone, thy love revealing
  But thy heart's deep loyalty.


Broad and liberal was thy judgment,
  One aim thine Equality
Caring not for creed or color,
  Man was man alike to thee.


If beyond this mortal striving,
  Man may reach a higher plain,
Thou wilt see Life's aim completed,
  And to greatest heights attain..

## Carney, The Brave Standard Bearer

'Twas a time of fiercest conflict,
 Enmity and awful woe,
'Twixt the North, the friend of Freedom,
 And the South, its bitter foe.

Day by day, the roar of battle
 Sounded forth its deathlike knell,
Day by day the best and bravest
 Died, amid the shot and shell.

Foremost in the ranks of warriors,
 Our black heroes took their place,
With the lines of fearless courage,
 Stamped upon each dusky face.

We recall with pride, the story
 Of the gallant Fifty-fourth,
Fighting on the field at Wagner,
 With the brave ones of the North.

There the dauntless William Carney,
 In the Union's sacred name,
Held aloft the flying colors,
 Won a never-dying fame.

He was first to plant the standard,
  On the fort he raised it high,
And he watched the floating banner,
  With a patriot's jealous eye.


Mid retreat and dire confusion,
  Oh! not once did he forget;
But he snatched the royal emblem
  From the lofty parapet.


On his knees he bravely followed,
  With one hand pressed to his side,
While the other, held the colors,
  Borne with patriotic pride.


What a cheer went up for Carney,
  As he held the colors high,
While a soldier's admiration,
  Beamed in every comrade's eye.


"Boys! I have but done my duty,"
  Carney said to those around,
"I have brought the old flag safely,
  And it never touched the ground."


'Twas a deed both brave and noble,
  And the loyal patriot's name,
Lives to-day and will forever,
  In our memories remain.

We can ne'er forget this hero,
  Or the gallant Fifty-Fourth,
Fighting on the field at Wagner,
  With the brave ones of the North.

---

## Unchained

### 1863

O'er the land, a hush had fallen,
  Hearts Thrilled expectantly,
Till from twice two million voices,
  Rang the glad cry, "We are free!"
Then the whole world caught the echo,
  "We are free! Yes! We are free!"

What a dawning from the midnight!
  What a day of jubilee!
Twas the New Year's song of triumph,
  That they sang so joyously,
Till it echoed and re-echoed
  "We are free! Yes! We are free!"

From the voice of one brave woman,
   Who, in human sympathy,
With a pen of love and pity
   Wrote the wrongs of slavery,
Came the glad new cry of triumph,
   "They are free! Yes! They are free!"


And the freedmen, still rejoicing,
   Sang of John Brown's victory,
Sang of Lincoln's Proclamation,
   Saying, "These have made us free."
Sumner, Garrison, and Phillips,
   All too fought to make us free.


Then the joyous song grew louder,
   By that price of loyalty,
Paid by us with our best lifeblood,
   We attest that we are free!
On the battle-field with honor,
   Our own blood has made us free."


Free indeed, but free to struggle,
   Free to toil unceasingly,
Naught of wealth, naught of possession,
   Was their portion, e'en tho' free;
But they faltered not, they failed not,
   Saying ever, "We are free!"

For their rightful place contending,
   They foresaw their destiny,
And they pleaded, never ceasing,
   "Give us opportunity!"
"Give us justice, recognition,
   'Tis our right! for we are free!"


From the lips of Frederic Douglass,
   Came these words of loyalty,
"Judge not harshly these my people,
   This is but their infancy,
From the depths they have ascended,
   Give them rights, for they are free!"


After years of ceaseless striving,
   Struggling for the mastery,
Over self and ill conditions,
   Still they're singing, "We are free!"
By the virtue of our struggle,
   We shall reap our destiny.


Though we suffer, in our freedom,
   By the hand of cruelty,
In the lawlessness of Evil,
   God is just, and we are free;
Life and love, not woe or slaughter,
   Are the birthright of the free.

When by predjudice untrammeled,
   Rich in manly liberty,
We receive that recognition
   Rightly given to the free,
Then the whole world shall proclaim it,
   "Free indeed! Yes! Ye are free!"

---

## A Hero of San Juan Hill

Among the sick and wounded ones,
   This stricken soldier-boy lay
With glassy eye and shortened breath,
   His life seemed slipping fast away.

My heart grew faint to see him thus,
   His dark brown face so full of pain,
I wondered if the mother's eyes
   Were looking for her boy in vain.

I bent to catch his feeble words;
   "I am so ill, and far from home,
I feel so strange and lonely here,
   You seem a friend, I'm glad you've come."

"I want to tell you how our boys
  Went charging on the enemy,
'Twas when we climbed up San Juan's Hill
  And there we got the victory."


"The Spaniards poured a heavy fire,
  We met it with a right good-will,
We saw the 71st fall back,
  And then our boys went up the hill."


"Yes up the hill, and gained it too,
  Not one brave boy was seen to lag;
Old Glory o'er us floating free,
  We'd gladly died for that old flag."


His dim eye brightened as he spoke,
  He seemed unconscious of his pain,
In fancy on the battle-field,
  He lived that victory o'er again.


And I, I seemed to grasp it too,
  The stalwart form, the dusky face,
Of each black hero climbing up,
To win fair glory for their race.

The Spaniards said, "That phalanx seemed
  To move like one black solid wall."
They flung defiance back at death,
  To answer to their country's call.

They fought for Cuban liberty,
  Up San Juan Hill they fought their way,
Until their life-blood freely spent,
  Marked how these heroes won the day.

March on dark sons of Afric's race,
  Naught can be gained by standing still,
Retreat not, quit yourselves like men,
  And like these heroes, climb the hill.

Till pride and predjuice shall cease,
  Till racial barriers are unknown,
Attain the heights, and thou shalt find,
  Equality upon the Throne.

## Wendell Phillips

A mighty tempest swept the Nation's course
And strong men sank beneath the ruthless blast
And feared to rise amid the wreck and ruin
Of Slave-bound misery and woe,
Nor dared to rally to the Call of Right,
Yet still despising the ignoble reign
Of Serfdom and its pitiless design
  Upon man's helpless brother-man.


O, direful was the need in that sad hour
And blessed was the sound of that rare voice
Of those strong words of challenge and demand
To save a Nation from itself.
Full willingly this tender sapling bowed,
Yet did not break beneath the weight of scorn,
Beneath the hatred of his fellow-man
  Nor would not hold his peace.


How mightily he rose amid the ruin,
Amid the blighting blast of Slavery's power,
And wrought, full hopeful of the righteous end,
Until the souls of men revived
And caught a vision of the better way,
The nobler standard of a Nation's might,
The consciousness of human brotherhood,
  The priceless boon of liberty.

O, heart of love! thine was the fine desire
To aid thy helpless brother in his need,
To teach thy kind the error and the shame
Of holding back another's right.
May we, whose chafing fetters were unbound
By thine outspoken word of strong defence,
Keep burning on the altar of our souls
    The incense of thy sacrifice.

# The Moaning

of

# The Tide

# To the Memory
## of
## Paul Lawrence Dunbar

Dunbar is dead! O Grief, thy cloud of gloom
   Hangs o'er his race! They sorely needed him,
That he should pass from them in his bright bloom
   Hath sorrowed deep; and troubled eyes are dim
With tears. To hear no more the voice that thrilled;
   To know his pen lies useless, undisturbed;
To know that evermore his songs are stilled,
   Hath filled their hearts with mournings, yet unheard.
O Singer-Artist, thy sweet tuneful lays
   Shall live, e'en though thy spirit swift hath flown
Back to its Maker; still we prize and praise
   The picture that thy skillful hand has thrown
Upon Life's canvass, that so well portrays
   The lot of him who close to Nature clings;
The joy, the pain, the pleasure of his days
   In field and cabin, where he weeps or sings;
It must be that thy soul-inspired Art
   Hath found, at last, in a diviner sphere
Its proper place, from earthly ills apart,
   To make complete its rare beginning here.

# To the Memory

## of

## William Lloyd Garrison

The Autumn leaves, rich golden-tinted leaves,
  Have fallen, and all barren lie the fields,
For, t'is the Reaping-time, when full-grown sheaves
  Are gathered in, and kindly Nature yields
Her choicest gifts, while Nature's children share
  The Autumn Glory, flooding vale and hill,
And thus the man, with life so full, so rare,
  Ripe, in his Autumn time, sleeps calm and still.


How fearlessly, how fervently he wrought!
  While from his lips fell truth like scattered grain,
Enriching all the field of human thought,
  Restoring faith to human hearts again.


Now, o'er our memories the mellow glow,
  Of all his love, of all his words and deeds
Shines brightly, and t'is ours to feel and know
  That he who pled our cause, who knew our needs
Has left with with us the golden-tinted leaves
  Of hope, such hope as made his life complete,
That we, like him may bring our Autumn sheaves,
  And lay them at the Master-Reaper's feet.

# The Brightening

## of the

# Hearth-Side

# The Yule-Tide Song

## A Christmas Legend

Away in the mystical land of the Orient, there lived an ancient people who worshipped the Gift of Song, and they also believed that certain souls were chosen to minister to humanity through its power, but, first of all, such souls must have passed through so much of human sorrow, until it glorified their countenance, and none but the Infinite One could read the mystery of that Glory.

At every Yule-tide season, it was their special mission to go forth among the people, even across the great waters, and to wait until the inspiration came upon them, and, wherever they might be, the song would find its way into the hearts of those who were hesitating or faltering in their duty toward their fellowmen, and the words of the song would be sweetly strange to its hearers, but the beauty of its music would be unlike that of any earthly strain, and its force would be so compelling that man would clearly see his path of duty. Then the Singer, his mission accomplished, would depart silently from among them, until another Yule-tide should lead him forth once more.

It was the Christmas-tide, and the heart of the great American city was beating and throbbing with restless eagerness, as the people hurried to and fro, each, in his own way, preparing for the morrow, the Sacred Day when Heaven's princely Gift, the Christ-Child, was offered human-kind.

The lights of the city gleamed and flashed, revealing too often the sight of misery, as weary, disheartened men, women and half-fed children of the poor, sought shelter from the chilling winds of the night.

From a small, low building, on one of the streets of that city where the endless row of ill-assorted tenement houses told of want and suffering, came the sound of mingled voices, and, a stranger, in passing, paused for a moment to listen, at the same time, catching sight of the word "Welcome" over its narrow doorway.

Unhesitatingly, he entered quietly, and seated himself among a mixed company of men, women and children.

The people gathered there represented that part of humanity who were too poor even to offer the simplest gifts, one to the other, but they had gathered there to hear the comforting words of the silvery-haired woman as she told the story of the Christ-Child, and this woman's soul went out in infinite longing, love, and pity, to these poor children of men.

The stranger sat entranced, unmindful of the covert glances of those around him.

It was small wonder that they sought to view him closely, for the expression of his bronze, foreign face, so peaceful in its repose, yet so striking in its clear-cut outlines, seemed to weave around them a spell of enchantment from which they were powerless to withdraw.

Across the aisle from him, sat a young girl of eighteen years, and beside her, a little child looking up into her face, pleading to be taken home with her, for this child's mother and father had passed into the Land of Silence, and their little one knew not where to lay its head.

The girl sat struggling within herself. Should she take this homeless child to her meagre abode, when she herself could barely live on the small pittance she received from her daily toil? No she could not. Again the little face looked up into hers, and again she struggled within herself. The child was homeless, friendless. O, what could she do when she herself was so bereft of daily needs!

Behind her sat a woman who had drank from the cup of disappointment and sorrow. These had overshadowed her life, and she questioned. What have I to offer others, when my own soul knows no peace?

The silvery-haired woman had ceased speaking, and drawn by the eager face of the stranger, she courteously addressed him, saying, "Friend, our strangers are always welcome among us. Have you a word of Yule-tide cheer?" And the stranger, rising and moving gracefully forward, answered in tones that thrilled the people into perfect silence, "Nay, I cannot find the word that I would speak, though much I thank you for this kindness to an unknown guest, but, there is a power within me that bids me give to you freely of that for which I came, but I must wait in silence until I shall be bidden to fulfill my mission." He ceased speaking, and stood with uplifted eyes, as if in quest of a divine commission. The people sat in awed silence, never had they seen a face like unto his before! Who was this mysterious stranger, and why stood he thus in this silence, that they could not comprehend?

The woman who had tasted the cup of human sorrow leaned forward and quietly whispered to the girl of eighteen years, "He is inspired, and I feel that when the moment comes, he will give to us his message."

Suddenly, as if in answer to her waiting, the singer

broke forth into the sweetest song that man could ever hear, and, the words, although unknown to them, were fraught with strange sweet meaning to their waiting souls, and somehow, they knew he sang of love divine, man's service unto man, of duty, seen and lovingly performed, of sacrifice, and best of all, the final benediction of Heaven's unbroken peace.

O, the strains of music were passing sweet, unlike that of any earthly strain, and as they looked upon the Singer, they saw his face was glorified with a halo, not of earth. Sweetly the marvellous Song died away, and moving silently forward, the Singer passed out into the night, they knew not whither.

But the song had filled its mission. The silvery-haired woman bowed her head in humble gratitude for the blessings of the hour.

Over the soul of the woman who had tasted human sorrow, came a great wave of peace, and the girl of eighteen years, ceased her struggling, and clasping close to her breast, the friendless child, hurried homeward through the night.

The Gift of Song worshipped by those Ancient People had indeed come to them. The Singer had vanished and according to the beautiful legend, whether or not he came from, or had returned to the Land of the Orient, we know not, we cannot say, we only know that the Singer and the Song had filled their Yule-tide Mission.

# The Burning Logs of Memory

## 𝔅e 𝔉aitbful

At the gate of the dear old homestead,
With hands clasped in lingering farewell,
We stood together in silence,
With feelings no language could tell,
As I looked in the face before me,
With its crown of silver gray hair,
I could see 'neath the lines of sorrow,
The image of Christ printed there.

Just a moment before, in her dwelling,
We had knelt together in prayer,
We had felt the peace of His presence,
And we knew that the Saviour was there.
And now came the moment of parting,
Standing there at the quaint rustic gate,
And somehow we felt but one impulse,
And that was to linger and wait,

For our hearts were too full for expression,
So we looked at each other and smiled,
And she with a voice firm, yet tender,
Said, "Be faithful, be faithful my child,
Remember the dear mother sleeping,
In the churchyard there by the road,
Oh, remember she gave you her blessing,
E're she entered her final abode."

Oh, remember she pled with the Father,
To keep you, her child in His care,
And to bring you at least to His Kingdom,
And she would be waiting there.
And He will my dear if you're faithful,
And then with a tear in her eye,
She whispered once more, "Oh, be faithful,"
God bless you my child, now, "Good-bye."


Good-bye! I could scarcely repeat it,
As I slowly turned from the place,
And I cast a longing glance backward,
For a glimpse of the dear old face.
And there she was standing, still smiling,
And waving her dear withered hand,
While I in return smiled bravely,
With emotions I scarce could command.


Then I turned and lingered a moment,
At the churchyard there by the road,
And I thought of the dear Sainted mother,
Resting now at home with her God.
Beyond lay the broad sparkling river,
Clear as crystal its bright waters shone,
And I thought of another we read of,
Winding its way by God's Throne.

Then I hastened once more on my journey,
Out into the world with its care,
Out into the world's temptations,
Which I knew were waiting me there.
But somehow new strength seemed given,
To battle and strive against sin,
And somehow I felt I should conquer,
And at last the victory win.

Be faithful, I hear the words ringing,
With sweetness, down, down through the years,
Giving hope in my hours of darkness,
Dispelling my doubts and my fears.
Oft in fancy I see the dear one,
As she looked in my face and smiled,
Oft in fancy I hear her soft whisper,
Oh, be faithful, be faithful my child.

## Palm Branches

In the hush of the Sabbath evening,
The people were wending their way,
To worship in God's own temple,
Where so often, they met to pray.
They had said like the Psalmist David,
"Let us go to the House of the Lord,
We're athirst for the living water,
And we long to feed on His word."

So they entered His sacred dwelling,
And they sat in silence there,
While the man of God bowed humbly,
And offered a fervent prayer.
That the peace of the Holy Spirit
Might enter each waiting soul,
That some weary wounded seeker,
Might believe and be made whole.

And the people's hearts grew tender,
As they heard the earnest prayer,
And their souls rejoiced within them,
For the Comforter was there;
Then followed the Holy Communion,
That Ordinance so divine,
And they ate of the bread, His body,
And they drank of His blood, the wine.

[ 102 ]

'Twas an hour of earnest devotion,
'Mid the hush and the holy calm,
Bringing its rest to the weary,
To the wounded, its healing balm.
Then a burst of heavenly music,
Broke over the stillness again,
And the sweet familiar "Palm Branches,"
Rang out in triumphant strain.


Louder and louder swelling,
Till it echoed with richness untold,
Till it seemed that the Master was coming,
As he did in the days of old.
When He rode as a king in triumph,
Through the streets of Jerusalem,
And they cast their garments before Him,
And proclaimed Him the "Ruler of Men."


And to-night the people adoring,
Gave honor to Him above,
And they brought Him, each one an offering,
The beautiful palms of love.
While the rich full strains of music,
So sweetly their spirits controlled,
Till it seemed that the Hosts of Heaven,
Were striking their Harps of gold.

And bowing in praise before Him,
Crying, "Holy, thrice Holy our Lord,
As they stood on the banks of the River,
Which flows by the bright Throne of God,
And the people waited enraptured,
For the last faint echo to cease,
Then arose and passed from His temple,
And went on their way in peace.

They were glad like the Psalmist David,
That they went to the House of the Lord,
They had drank from the Living Waters,
They had fed on His precious Word,
In their souls the strain of Palm Branches,
Seemed to linger and gently abide,
They remembered with joy its sweetness,
In the hush of that even-tide.

## The Organist's Dream

Yes, I know I am a stranger,
But when you came in that door,
I just felt that I could trust you,
Though we've never met before,
That white ribbon you are wearing,
Somehow makes me want to say,
Something that's been pressing on me,
It has troubled me all day.

Thanks! I knew that you would listen,
When I saw your bow of white,
So I'll just begin and tell you,
Of a dream I had last night.
It was strange that I should dream it,,
For my dreams are very few,
But this seemed to be so real,
And I hope it won't come true.

I was in a great tall building,
Shut up in a dark, dark room,
And the darkness was so fearful,
That it seemed like mid-night gloom,
And I prayed, and begged, and pleaded,
For some friend to let me out,
But in vain my cries and pleading,
I was doomed without a doubt.

Then I ceased to call and listen,
For I heard sweet voices sing,
And their tones grew loud and louder,
Till they made the arches ring,
With these words that they were singing,
There is no more room in Heaven,
And to him who strays and wanders,
Entrance there shall not be given.


Ah! I thought of dear Old England,
How I've made the organ ring,
In the old church on the corner,
How the choir used to sing,
I have heard the sweetest music,
I have played the sweetest songs,
Grand old airs from Hayden Handel,
Music that has stirred the throngs.


But last night those voices singing,
"There is no more room in Heaven,
And to him who strays and wanders,
Entrance there shall not be given,"
Made me ask myself the question,
Is there no more room for me?
Am I shut outside of Heaven,
Now and for Eternity?

Then I prayed again and pleaded,
Begged that I might be released,
But they heeded not my pleading,
And the voices never ceased.
Singing, no more room in heaven,
And I knew I was denied,
Entrance through the Heavenly Portal,
I alone was shut outside.

All night long I heard the singing,
And the words were just the same,
And to tell the truth about it,
I was glad when morning came,
But somehow I can't help thinking,
That perhaps I'd ought to pray,
For I haven't heard a sermon,
Or a prayer for many a day.

Though I promised the dear mother
That I'd go to meeting some,
But it's been five years and over,
Since I left the dear old home.
And I haven't kept my promise,
But that dream I had last night,
Makes me feel ashamed and sorry,
That I haven't done just right.

Yes, I know I should be better,
And I'm really going to try,
For I've been so wild and reckless,
That I'm hardly fit to die,
But you've made me feel more cheerful,
For your words have been so kind,
And somehow the burden's lifted,
That was pressing on my mind.

Well, Good-bye, I'm glad I met you,
And I'll do just as you say,
I will write the dear old mother,
That her boy has learned to pray,
And although I've strayed and wandered,
Though I've lived so carelessly,
I will try to enter Heaven,
For I know there's room for me.

# Dreams

## By The

# Driftwood Fire

## A Dream of the New Year

Through the waning hours and moments,
Of the slowly dying year,
I sat watching, watching, waiting,
For the New Dawn to appear.
While the Old Year's strife and struggle,
Like a swiftly flowing stream,
Passed before me till I wearied,
Fell asleep—asleep to dream.

That I saw a lofty castle,
Vast in size, and wondrous bright,
And I stood outside its portals,
Waiting for the dawning light.
From its towers the bells were ringing,
In a strange discordant tone,
Wailing out their mournful measures,
Like a mortal's dying moan.

Still I waited, knocked and waited,
Lingered through the shadowed night,
For I longed to learn the secret
Of this castle, vast and bright.
Till a voice within, cried loudly,
"Thou shalt have that wish sublime,
Thou art knocking at Life's castle,
And the Keeper's name is Time."

"And the bells you hear above you,
Ring out all the dying years,
Ring out Man's past griefs and sorrows,
Ring out blasted hopes and fears.
With the coming of the New Year,
They will cease their sad refrain,
You will hear them chiming sweetly,
Ringing out a joyous strain.


Watch and wait awhile with patience,
Wait with hope, and not in fear,
For the New Year swift approaches,
Its bright dawning draweth near."
So I waited, watched and waited
Till the castle's door swung wide,
And the keeper bade me enter,
Saying, "Mortal, here abide."


'Twas indeed a wondrous castle,
With its arches gleaming bright,
E'en the keeper's face was beaming,
With a rare and radiant light,
Through the spacious halls, he led me
Over floors of spotless white,
Till it seemed that mortal vision
Ne'er beheld a fairer sight.

On its walls in blazoned letters,
I could trace each written line,
And the words were wrought most strangely,
Words no mortal could define.
And the keeper softly speaking,
Read them, one by one to me;
"Resolution, Faith and Duty,
Hope and Opportunity."


Then I asked him, "Can you tell me
Why these written words appear?"
He replied, "These are the watchwords
That shall guide thee through the year,
Just resolve to do thy duty,
Thine the opportunity,
Hope shall aid thee, in thy purpose,
Do it well and faithfully."


Then the bells pealed out so loudly,
Ringing out their joyous strain
That I started from my slumbers,
Found myself alone again.
Saw no more Life's wondrous castle,
Vanished now the keeper, Time,
Heard no more the joyful pealing
Of the bell's sweet, tuneful chime.

Day had dawned, the night was over,
Life's old year was safely past,
Now had come a brighter morning,
Life's New Year had dawned at last.
But the dream had filled its mission,
Made my path of duty clear,
Hope and Faith were now the watchwords,
Brightening up my glad New Year.

## The Plains of Peace

Again my fancy takes its flight,
And soars away on thoughtful wing,
Again my soul thrills with delight,
And this the fancied theme, I sing,
From Earthly scenes awhile, I find release,
And dwell upon the restful Plains of Peace.


The Plains of Peace are passing fair,
Where naught disturbs and naught can harm,
I find no sorrow, woe or care,
These all are lost in perfect calm,
Bright are the joys, and pleasures never cease,
For those who dwell on the Plains of Peace.


No scorching sun or blighting storm,
No burning sand or desert drear,
No fell disease or wasting form,
To mar the glowing beauty here.
Decay and ruin ever must decrease,
Here on the fertile, healthful Plains of Peace.

What rare companionship I find,
What hours of social joy I spend,
What restfulness pervades my mind,
Communing with congenial friend.
True happiness seems ever to increase,
While dwelling here upon the Plains of Peace.


Ambitions too, are realized,
And that which I have sought on earth,
I find at last idealized,
My longings ripen into worth,
My fondest hopes no longer fear decease,
But bloom forth brightly on the Plains of Peace.


'Tis by my fancy, yet 'tis true,
That somewhere having done with Earth,
We shall another course pursue,
According to our aim or worth,
Our souls from mortal things must find release,
And dwell immortal on the Plains of Peace.

## Her Offering

Lay aside your pen for a moment,
And listen, my dear to me,
While I tell you a strange, sweet story,
The sweetest that ever could be.
And perhaps, the theme will inspire you
And perhaps you will catch the strain
Of sweetness, and maybe you'll write it
When you take up your pen again.

So, there in the evening twilight,
I gladly laid down my pen
And listened to hear her story,
As sweet to me now, as then.
It was just at the close of daylight,
When shadows begin to unfold,
I remember the time so clearly,
And this was the story she told,—

Last night, my dear, in dreamland,
I sat in a princely hall,
And its arches were solid marble,
Its pillars stately and tall,
I saw before me an altar,
Exquisitely wrought in gold,
And the white-robed priest behind it,
Was saying, my people behold,—

To-day is the great passover,
Of thanks and of sacrifice,
Give ye of your best and purest,
The least of these will suffice.
Come then with sincerest devotion,
Bring all that ye can afford,
Oh, who will be first to offer
Thanksgiving and praise to the Lord?


Down the aisle of the princely dwelling,
Two maidens in spotless white,
Came bearing rich treasures of silver,
Their faces beaming with light.
And, ascending the steps to the altar,
They offered their gifts to the Lord,
They had brought Him the best and the purest.
The richest each one could afford.


Just behind them in humble submission,
A woman came, weary and worn,
With feeble, faltering, foot-steps,
With garments so faded and torn,
In her hand she was tenderly bearing,
Two tiny pieces of bread,
And, ascending the steps to the altar,
She bowed, and tremblingly said,—

"Not a morsel of food have I tasted,
Since yesterday's early dawn,
But I've waited, Oh, earnestly waited,
For the coming of this bright morn,
This is all that I have to offer,
This simple gift to the Lord,
It's the best that I have and the purest.
The richest that I can afford."


And the white-robed priest said softly,
"Your gift will indeed suffice,
In truth you have kept the passover,
Of thanks and sacrifice."
And then, as the priest was speaking,
The scene faded slowly away,
And the princely hall had vanished.
I awoke to find it was day.


"So, my dear I have told the story,
And I hope you have caught the strain,
Of sweetness,—and now I leave you,
Good-night, till we meet again."
And there in the evening twilight,
I gladly took up my pen,
And I wrote this strange, sweet story,
As sweet to me now, as then.

# My Dream of Long Ago

### (TO MY AUNT)

I had a strange sweet dream long, long ago,
When in my years I yet was but a child,
And oft since then as I have dreamed it o'er
Its sweetness has my saddest hours beguiled.

It was that she who like my mother seemed
And I had travelled far and travelled long,
Her hand and mine together tightly clasped,
She with a thoughtful look, and I with song.

And walking thus our way led pleasantly
Mid winding paths on either side where grew
Rare flowers, their perfumes wafted on the breeze,
Which all around us their rich fragrance threw.

But soon our road turned suddenly aside,
Where rose a height of stony rugged ground,
No flowers bloomed upon this hilly waste,
Where sighing winds played mournfully around.

Below the hills, half-hidden, a tiny path
Went winding round and out into the road.
So smoothly did it keep its tiny way
It seemed a guide that nature had bestowed.

We paused, and she spoke there in tender tones,
"My child, you take the easy path around,
For I can better face the windy blast,
My feet can better tread the stony ground."

And I, who knew no will save hers alone,
Obeyed, and o'er the tiny pathway sped,
Oft looking up to see her bravely climb
The stony height with firm and steady tread.

And now the winds her garments roughly blew,
But she, unheeding their rude, blighting blast,
Pressed on, and when I from the pathway ran
We met, and hands again together clasped.

Before us stretched an endless smooth white road
Which ran beside the fairest verdant field
That ever mortal eye had looked upon
Or ever Nature's storehouse had revealed.

Above our heads the sun shone brightly now,
It seemed to thrill our hearts with hope anew
And shed upon our path a mellow light
Which all around us a soft radiance threw.

Thus hand in hand we lightly trod along
This pleasant road with neither curve or bend
When I awoke to find it all a dream
And we had never reached our journey's end.

And yet it may be that this very road,
The end of which we vainly tried to trace,
Might still have led to pastures far more fair,
We might have found some peaceful resting place.

# A Floating Spar

## Hope

The driftwood fire burns brightly on, but dreaming-time is over. Stern reality sounds its convincing call to the time of our awakening.

Over the troubled waters of our civilization comes a human cry for human rights—a startling echo from the far cry of bondage over half a century ago.

Prejudice, the floating wreckage of chattel slavery, rises ever to the surface of the turbulent waters of a Nation's life, obstructing each best attempt toward a safe course to its highest citizenship.

The clanking chains of racial injustice, that bind and hold fast the infinite longings and fondest ambitions of a human soul, must be broken.

Doors that are closed against him who lives and breathes in this, a free Republic;—who battles for its preservation, who embraces its educational opportunities, who enters its arena with unswerving purpose to aid in its progressive interests by contributing his own thrift, industry, intellectual and spiritual activities—must be opened.

Had the artist of 50 years ago desired to paint a thrilling picture of human woes, he might have produced upon his canvass this painfully familiar scene

—the auction-block—the slaver—and the enslaved, and beneath he might have written these words:

"The Barrier to a Nation's Progress.."

But, if in the intensity of his soul, the artist of to-day desires to paint a true picture of the present attitude of the American mind toward a part of its citizenship, he might portray upon his canvass the following scene—an American citizen of darker hue, with manly bearing, standing, with outstretched hands before the closed door of a minature institution known as "Progressive Civilization," and behind him, a lawless mob. Beneath this he might well write the convincing words:

"Predjudice and Lynch Law—The Curse of the Twentieth Century."

But, happily, amid the wreckage, despite the turbulence, the floating spar of Hope is seen, making its way toward Right and Justice.

Julia Ward Howe beheld it, even through the gleaming camp-fires, when her soul longed for the "glory of the coming of the Lord." She saw its consummation in and through her mighty refrain, "His Cause is Marching On."

Harriet Beecher Stowe held fast to the firm support of Hope, in her vivid portrayal of Slavery, as a living dramatic reality, in that masterpiece of human history, "Uncle Tom's Cabin," and, it may be that her mantle will fall upon one who knows and feels the heart-throbs of his race, who has tatsted the bitterness of the bondage of American freedom and, who will yet write a great American Story, in which he shall tell of the Nation's greatest injustice, the denial of the ballot in the South; hc shall also reveal volcanic fires of predjudice in the North, over which we daily tread.

Happily for him, he shall weave into the fabric of his genius, the inherited originalities of his people, the development and power of their musical birthright, and the cheering influence of their native humor.

It may be that the romance of home and social life will add a touch of coloring to his narrative.

But the pathos of his story, and the intensity of his longings will be most deeply felt, when he writes of an unalterable faith in the ultimate triumph of justice and its equalizing power. Surely then shall the Nation's heart be touched, and the American conscience stirred to higher, nobler impulses.

O! floating Spar of Hope
'Tis ours to cling full fast to thee,
Outriding e'en the mighty wave,
And current, strong with black despair,
Not even these have power to engulf
Nor stay thine onward course.
Justice and Right are bearing down upon us,
Ay, holding out strong hands,
Of help and timely rescue.
They lead to that long-looked-for Haven
Where man at last plays fair with brother-man
And gives him back his ancient Right.
                    Equality!

# ON THE LONG
# ISLAND INDIAN

How relentless, how impartial,
Is the fleeting hand of time,
By its stroke, great empires vanish
Nations fall in swift decline.

Once resounding through these forests,
Rang the warwhoop shrill and clear,
Once here lived a race of Red Men,
Savage, crude, but knew no fear.

Here they fought their fiercest battles,
Here they caused their wars to cease,
Sitting round their blazing camp fires,
Here they smoked the Pipe of Peace.

Tall and haughty were the warriors,
Of this fierce and warlike race.
Strong and hardy were their women,
Full of beauteous, healthy grace.

Up and down these woods they hunted,
Shot their arrows far and near.
Then in triumph to their wigwams,
Bore the slain and wounded deer.

"On the Long Island Indian" appeared in *The Annual Report of the Montauk Tribe of Indians for the Year 1916* (31 Aug., 1916), and is reproduced in this volume by courtesy of the Library of Anthropology at the Nassau County Museum, Sands Point Preserve, Port Washington, NY.

Thus they dwelt in perfect freedom,
Dearly loved their native shores,
Wisely chose their Chiefs or Sachems,
Made their own peculiar laws.

But there came a paler nation
Noted for their skill and might.
They aroused the Red Man's hatred,
Robbed him of his native right.

Now remains a scattered remnant
On these shores they find no home,
Here and there in weary exile,
They are forced through life to roam.

Just as Time with all its changes
Sinks beneath Oblivion's Wave,
So today a mighty people
Sleep within the silent grave.

# PUBLISHED WORKS:
## PLAY, ESSAYS
### *1900–1932*

❧ ❧ ❧

# MEMORIES OF CALVARY
## AN EASTER SKETCH

## PREFACE

It is the writer's strong conviction that more and more the need for strong faith in Christ, as the Redeemer of men, impresses itself upon those who seek not only for Spiritual Truth, but for Spiritual Peace as well.

The many doctrines of the present day, the rapid advance of materialism all tend to detract from rather than add to spiritual strength, and the writer believes that the recognition of Christ, as the Highest Ideal is imperative and absolutely needful for man's best development.

OLIVIA WARD BUSH

## CHARACTERS

NIGHT *(personified)—a young woman wearing a long black robe, trimmed with stars.*

ANXIOUS SEEKER—*(a young woman who seeks to know the truth of Calvary's Cross, wearing first black, then white).*

MALE QUARTETTE *(invisible).*

HERALDS OF THE CROSS—*(15 or 20 young men and young women, who herald the Easter morn; white robes are preferred).*

Originally published in Philadelphia by the A.M.E. Book Concern, c. 1917. Reproduced in this volume by courtesy of the Harris Collection of American Poetry and Plays, John Hay Library, Brown University, Providence, RI.

# MEMORIES OF CALVARY

## SCENE 1

### Night on Calvary

*Tall palms may be used on platform arranged to suggest a grove—lights are turned off or dimly seen. In the distance, on an elevation, is seen a wooden Cross, at the base of which kneels or sits the Anxious Seeker, robed in black.*

*Night appears robed in black and silver stars. Night soliloquizes, comforts Anxious Seeker, then departs. Anxious Seeker soon follows.*

*Before curtain rises invisible male quartette sings the familiar hymn, "Peace, Perfect Peace."*

VOICE OF NIGHT  *(Soliloquizes).* Day has long since departed, over the sleeping earth, silence has fallen and the restless heart of man beats calm again in these, his slumbering hours, while there on Calvary's Hill stands out the cross and though Earth's shadows cast their endless lengths over all the vast expanse of the Creator's earth, they cannot hide from view this sacred emblem of man's imperishable immortal inheritance, they cannot dim the greatness of its glory.

But as for man, he sleeps, for he is a weary, poor, restless man, ever weary, yet ever striving, seeking always, yet still unsatisfied. He has traversed the earth from shore to shore, laying low the mighty forests in his pathway, holding back the onward course of rushing waters, awearied, yes, but relentless in his search for greater triumphs.

Deep down into the heart of Mother-Earth he has forged his way and brought up priceless gems from Nature's richest mines. Down into the almost unfathomable depths of mighty oceans he has laid his cable lengths, bringing near the distant lands, enabling man to send with speed a message to his far off brother man. He has hewn his way through mighty rocks of unnumbered ages. He has scaled the mountain even to its highest peak and builded there his magnificent palaces of home. Awearied? Yes, but not content, he needs must try the unknown regions up and beyond the floating clouds, and out of the mighty power of his mental concept, he has wrought the wonder of the centuries—the chariots of the air—by which men fly at will to heights such as man ne'er before conceived of.

But man's soul is not at rest, for, over and beyond his great achievements, stands out the Cross of Christ, the mortal and immortal Emblem of man's highest need and strongest hope.

O Calvary! Calvary! in thee, and thee alone shall man find peace and rest. *(Discovers Anxious Seeker at the foot of Cross.)*

But who is this in mournful guise beneath the Shadow of the Cross? Speak Mortal! Why art thou here in this, the gloom and darkness of Earth's silent hour? The Voice of Night now bids thee speak! What seekest thou?

ANXIOUS SEEKER.—O Voice of Night, I seek to know the meaning of this Cross: my soul is weighted down with longing for the higher way of life, and I did feel that, somehow here, beneath this Cross, my soul might find release, and I must here abide until the morning breaks. Dost thou know the meaning of this Cross?

VOICE OF NIGHT.—O Anxious Seeker, 'tis the Cross of Christ, and beneath it is the Mount of Calvary. Have you not heard the wondrous story of Him, who suffered there and died?

ANXIOUS SEEKER.—Ah! Yes the story has been told, yet I, alas! but darkly can discern its meaning. O, tell me aught you know of Calvary's Christ.

VOICE OF NIGHT.—O Anxious Seeker, in the days when man first felt the need of Life and help Divine, I looked from out my home, amid the shining stars, and I beheld on Calvary's Hill the Cross, where hung the Crucified, who gave His Life a ransom for man's sin. I saw the veil of the Mighty Temple rent in twain, I heard His agonizing cry. It is finished! It is finished! I heard the cry of mortals in their terror and their fears. But once again I looked, and Lo! the Cross was bare. The Christ had filled His mighty purpose. Through the vaulted heavens above my starry home I heard Angelic hosts proclaim: The Christ has risen! Behold! man's fettered soul is now redeemed forevermore. O, Anxious Seeker, have but faith and thou shalt truly find the Prince of Peace. And now, the morning breaks! Farewell, and when we meet again, may you have changed your robe of gloom for one of spotless white. Farewell! Farewell!

*(Night disappears and lights are turned on gradually.)*

ANXIOUS SEEKER.—The Prince of Peace! Ah! now the light comes in: I feel His Kingly Presence in my soul! The Cross stands out in all its brightness now, and from the distance comes the sound of heavenly music, as if 'twere borne on Angel's wings. *(Listens.)*

INVISIBLE MALE QUARTETTE *sings the familiar hymn.*

> Jesus calls us o'er the tumult
> Of our Life's wild, restless sea,
> Day by day his sweet voice soundeth,
> Saying Christian, follow Me!
>
> Jesus calls us, by Thy mercies,
> Saviour, may we hear Thy call,
> Give our hearts to Thy obedience,
> Serve and love Thee best of all!

ANXIOUS SEEKER.—Ah! how sweetly strange this music seems, as if in answer to my soul's desire. I will arise, I will put off this robe of gloom for one of spotless white to greet the Easter Dawn.

*(Anxious Seeker departs and lights are turned on in full.)*

## SCENE II

### Easter Morning

*Lights are turned on full. Heralds of the Cross enter bearing flowers to cast at the foot of Cross. They sing, Holy! Holy! Holy! Lord God Almighty. Enter Anxious Seeker (robed in white). She joins them in praise. They depart together singing, All hail the power of Jesus' Name.*

*(Enter 15 or 20 young men and women. "Heralds of the Cross," robed in white: they approach the Cross and scatter flowers at its base, singing Holy! Holy! Holy! Lord God Almighty. They continue to sing until the Anxious Seeker returns and lays her flowers at the base of Cross. Then rising, she turns to the singers.)*

ANXIOUS SEEKER.—O glad young voices, heralding this blessed morn, I, too, would seek to praise the Prince of Peace, for He has passed my way, and from His storehouse rich with love, has showered blessings on my waiting soul.

O listen, while I give to you the wondrous messages of His love. *(Recites the following verses):*

ANXIOUS SEEKER.—

> Stealing over my heart with such sweetness,
>     Came the words so divinely true:
> "I will open the windows of Heaven,
>     And pour rich blessings on you."
> He did open the windows of Heaven,
>     And oh, such a blessing He poured;
> My Father, so rich in His mercies,
>     My Saviour, my King, and my Lord.

I had asked Him in pitiful weakness,
    To lead me, in this, my way;
It was night, in my soul, as I pleaded,
    But He led me to perfect day.
Out into the broad green pastures,
    Of which I had little dreamed;
Out into the bright clear sunshine,
    Where the rays of His Glory gleamed.

Ah, the blessing was more than He promised,
    For it seemed I could scarcely contain
The wonderful flow of His mercies
    I could only whisper His name.
And praise Him for what He had given,
    His promise so sweet and true,
"I will open the windows of Heaven
    And pour rich blessings on you."

HERALDS OF THE CROSS *reply:*

We do rejoice with Thee
    In this, Thy new-found peace,
Come blend your voice with ours
    In highest praise.

*All retire from stage, headed by Anxious Seeker, singing "All hail the power of Jesus' Name." They sing until their voices sound as if in the distance.*
    *Curtain falls.*

*Note—One of the following Easter poems might be used between the two scenes and one might be used at conclusion of Memories of Calvary.*

# THE CRUCIFIED

Night's Shadows wrapped the Cross in gloom,
    And e'en the shining stars grew dim with grief;

All Nature bowed in agony,
   And yearned in silent anguish for relief.
The Temple's Veil was rent in twain,
   The dead, though sleeping through the quiet years,
Arose, and walked the troubled Earth
   While living souls grew faint with many fears.
What can this mighty tumult mean?
   The Christ, the suffering Saviour now has died!
Ask not, but gaze on yonder Mount
   Of Calvary, where hangs the Crucified!

OLIVIA WARD BUSH

## AN EASTER ECHO

Easter dawned, but I was weary
   With the fever and the pain,
And my soul within seemed sinking,
   Never to revive again.

This affliction pressed me sorely,
   "Oh, if Fate would just be kind
And relieve my tortured being,
   That my soul might be resigned."

"O, that peace would follow conflict,
   O, that grief would turn to joy,
O, that suffering might conquer
   Where it threatens to destroy."

"Ah! if I could catch a vision
   Of the risen Christ today,
I am sure my faith would strengthen,
   And all doubt would pass away."

Thus with self I lay communing,
   Tossing, restless, in my pain,
When, within my room came stealing
   Softly breathing, this sweet strain—

Sung by little children's voices,
  Heralding our Easter day;
Ringing through my open window
  From God's Temple o'er the way.

"He is Risen! He is Risen!
  Wipe away your falling tear,
Pain and grief and doubt are vanquished,
  For the Lord Christ draweth near."

Hushed at once was my complaining,
  And my earthly sight grew dim,
For my soul had caught a vision,
  And rejoicing, cried to Him,—

Who today arose in triumph,
  "O, Thou Conqueror of strife,
I accept Thy heaven-sent message,
  Let it echo through my life,—

Till it overrules all weakness,
  Till it crushes doubt and fear,
Till I say in Death, victorious,
  He, the Lord Christ draweth near.

Years have passed and still the echo
  Lingers with assuring ring,
E'en in pain or sore affliction,
  Children's voices seem to sing:

"He is risen! He is risen!
  Wipe away your falling tear,
Pain and grief and doubt are vanquished,
  For the Lord Christ draweth near."

OLIVIA WARD BUSH

# AND I, IF I BE LIFTED UP

He giveth songs way in the night,
  He listens when His children pray;
He makes it bright as noontide light,
  He turneth darkness into day.

I heard His voice at midnight hour,
    It came so sweet and tenderly:
And I, if I be lifted up,
    Will surely draw all men to Me.

And I beheld Him on the Cross,
    Uplifted for my guilt and sin;
Uplifted there in love divine
    That He might draw all men to Him.
And I beheld Him once again,
    Uplifted as the Father's Son,
Uplifted in the realms above,
    A King upon a Kingly throne.

I fancied Heaven's pearly gates,
    Swung wide that I might enter in;
I fancied Heaven's arches rang,
    With praise for victory over sin.
And I beheld a white-robed host,
    Low at His feet, adoring fall.
I heard their grand triumphant song,
    He is our King, the Lord of all.

'Twas but His voice at midnight hour,
    Which came so sweet and tenderly;
And I, if I be lifted up,
    Will surely draw all men to me.
He gave me songs way in the night,
    I felt His joy and peace within,
He led toward Heaven my fancy's flight,
    That He might draw me close to Him.
                    OLIVIA WARD BUSH

# FOR THEE
## (An Easter Poem)

And from His hands and from His side,
    Flowed down great drops of blood;

For you, for me, for everyone,
　　Streamed out that crimson flood.
Take thou this comfort to thine heart,
　　Poor wounded, stricken soul,
That He who chastens thee with love,
Thy weakness will control.

If bitter is the cup you taste,
　　In dark Gethsemane;
Remember that He tasted first
　　That bitter cup for thee.
He'll move thy obstacle of sin,
　　He'll set thy spirit free,
He proved His endless boundless love,
　　On rugged Calvary.

Ah, trembling One, He did it all,
　　Because He loved thee so;
Then cast on Him this care of thine,
　　O, trust in Him, and know:
That from His hands and from His side,
　　Flowed down great drops of blood,
For you, for me, for everyone,
　　Streamed out that crimson flood.

　　　　　　　　Olivia Ward Bush


# WHY WEEPEST THOU?
## (Easter Poem)

"Why weepest thou here?" said the Master,
　　And whom dost thou seek today?
And Mary replied in her sorrow:
　　"Thy have taken my Lord away.

And I know not where they have laid Him,
　　Though I've watched since the early morn;

I would take Him away could I find Him,
   Oh, Sir! to whence was He borne."

And the Master with love overflowing,
   Said Mary, in accents so sweet,
That she knew her dear Master had spoken,
   And with joy she fell at His feet:
Wiped away were the tears of her sorrow,
   Her waiting had not been in vain.
In her soul rang the Angel's glad message:
   He arose, and He liveth again!

Why weepest thou here waiting Christian,
   Know ye not that He's risen today?
That the confines of earth could not hold Him,
   And the stone has been rolled away?
Have you waited and watched since the morning?
   Then your waiting has not been in vain,
List the voice of His Angel proclaiming,
   He arose, and He liveth again!

Why weepest thou too, trembling sinner,
   Know ye not of His power to save?
For thy sake over death He has triumphed
   For thy sake He arose from the grove.
Wipe away then the tears of thy sorrow,
   For your longings have not been in vain,
For thee is the Angel's glad message,
   He arose, and He liveth again!

OLIVIA WARD BUSH

# UNDERCURRENTS OF
# SOCIAL LIFE

Standing on the threshold of a new century, with its suggestive outlook for greater development in the material world, new and improved lines of thought, together with expansive moral and mental forces, every race, nation or people burns with an eager desire to meet the demands attendant upon the conditions of a new era.

Necessity requires that colored Americans conform to existing circumstances in accordance with their possibilities and capabilities.

While it is true that former years of enforced dependence on the favored race [have] interfered with, yet not totally destroyed, the needed consciousness of responsibility in us, and which is a requisite in the ever-changing constantly improving business world, there is a condition over which we have entire control, and for which we have individual agency, namely, Improved Social Law, which eventually must terminate in positive success in business life and moral attainments.

There is a fixed law in the natural order of things, that material and moral discoveries for the good of humanity have always their opposing and contradictory forces.

For instance, the social life of the present day is far more attractive than in past centuries, and we must admit that its

Originally published in the *Colored American Magazine* 2 (Dec. 1900): 155–56.

moral side has been largely cultivated, but its evils, too, have become greater in proportion with its improvement.

We bask in the glittering light and brilliant effect of the elegant surroundings, carefully designed to allure and dazzle the individual into complete unconsciousness of what the true life is, unmindful that the offered glass, with its sparking contents, is slowly yet surely sapping the foundation of our highest ambitions, fascinated with a few hours of pleasure, we participate again and again, until worthy desire is completely usurped by frivolity.

Confronted with one of the greatest problems of the day, and of which we are the central figure, it is the time for careful thought, guarded action, proper disposition of financial possession and the sacrifice of useless customs for combined effort in the all-absorbing issues which tend to our advancement.

Young men and women, let us arouse from this apathy and indifference, and if it be true that servitude has deterred us in material progress, now under an improved social law let us lay anew the foundation necessary to the success of any people which shall furnish moral incentives for real progress, and which shall reward decisive action with actual development.

# ECHOES FROM
# THE CABIN SONG

If the song-themes of the ages with their surging tides of human emotion could be portrayed in dramatic form, they would, undoubtedly, blend into an Immortal Rhapsody. They have come to us over the years of human experience, bringing the far-flung fragrances of the centuries. Some have been martial in their strains, other[s], songs of triumph, conquest and victory. How thrilling the chant of Miriam, the Israelite maiden:

> Sound the loud timbrel over Egypt's dark sea,
> Jehovah has triumphed, His people are free.

How stirring the strains of the "Marsellaise," "A Mighty Fortress is Our God," and [our] own "Battle Hymn of the Republic." Countless songs are eternally sacred to those, for whom, out of national experiences, they have been wrought.

The Cabin Songs, or Spirituals, borne in the cotton-fields of the Southland, and in the cabin home, when the day's toil was over, ring with varying notes of desire. They are not wholly sorrow-songs, altho' their joy-lines seem to echo a soul-cry. They are, noticeably, songs of hope, faith, alternate yearnings and rejoicings, beautiful in their imagery, rich in harmony, and they glorify the humble.

It is said that when the first Jubilee Singers visited Germany for the purpose of raising funds for Fiske University,

"Cultural Art" column, *Westchester Record-Courier*, (30 Apr. 1932).

a noted musician in Berlin, declared that "Out of the anguished souls of these people, have come these immortal songs—they are the passion-flowers of the blood of Martyrs."

The Cabin Song reveals, always a "moving element," so obviously expressed in the "fountain theme":

> I've just come from the fountain,
> I've just come from the fountain, Lord,
> I've just come from the fountain,
> And His Name is so sweet.

They also reach an ecstatic climax of praise, as in:

> Jesus fed me when I was hungry,
> Gave me drink when I was dry,
> Jesus clothed me when I was naked.
> Bless His Name! Bless His Name!

These songs evidence an in-born assurance of heavenly reward, and a joyous home-going, as expressed in the familiar lines:

> Swing low, sweet chariot,
> Comin' forth to carry me home, (etc.)

Outstanding among them is the Meditation Song, "Steal Away to Jesus," merging into a full acceptance of the fact that life must have its earthly ending. It may well be likened unto Alfred Tennyson's "Crossing the Bar." The Singer of the Cabin, looking out upon Nature, sees "Green Trees Blending, the flash of lightning, the roar of thunder," all of which blend into "one clear call" for him, while the "trumpet" of joy sounds within his soul, and he sings triumphantly:

> I ain't got long to stay here.

Echoes of this Great Symphony of human feelings, are continuously heard in the rich-toned voice of Colored Americans, who have immortalized their ancestral birthright, and today they are acclaimed nationally and internationally. Added to these, is an increasing number of youthful song-artists, as yet publicly unknown, who give evidence of rich possibilities, within the realm of song. Among them is a golden-voiced baritone, now living in the western part of our country. His youthful career, attended by seemingly insurmountable difficulties, calls forth sincere tributes of commendation, while his persistent endeavors to perfect his art, is already a source of inspiration to his fellow-artists. It is not surprising that, here in the east, our young Colored Americans are asking the question, "Who is this rare singer of the west?"

# ESSAY ON
# JOHN GREENE

John Greene of Chicago, Ill., is the inimitable song-artist, whose haunting tones echo, and re-echo with the musical inheritance of his people. He sings with deep intensity of feeling, his range from the power-note to soft cadences of tenderness and pathos, is overwhelmingly marvellous. His Art is distinctively a scenic process, revealing so vividly the varying experiences of human emotions, until the listener becomes keenly conscious of rare tonal interpretation, and also catches an inner vision of Life's realities, portrayed through the gift of song.

High reputable musical critics, national and international, have, unhesitatingly and unreservedly, named John Greene with Roland Hayes and Paul Robeson, in the realm of contributive art.

John Greene spent the early years of childhood in Columbus, Georgia, his birthplace.

In 1924, as a resident of Chicago, he began voice study, with George Garner, a widely-known singer. At the conclusion of six months, T. Theodore Taylor, a noted musician, became Mr. Greene's instructor under whose tutelage he remained until 1929. Later he was awarded a scholarship by the Cosmopolitan School of Music for one year, under the tutorship of Mr. Shireley M. K. Gandell. In 1930 he received a Rosenwald Fund Fellowship, which was repeated in

"Cultural Art" column, *Westchester Record-Courier*, (21 May 1932).

1931. In the summer of 1931 he was the first prize winner in a vocal contest sponsored by the Kraft Cheese Company of Chicago, Ill., in which over six hundred voices competed. Among his notable appearances were, his major recital in Chicago's Loop, and his successful program for the National Cash Register Company of Dayton, Ohio.

Mr. Greene has toured the State of North Carolina, singing in its Summer schools, for the state. He has received high tributes of commendation for his renditions in the following states: Ohio, West Virginia, Virginia, Missouri, Kentucky, New York, Wisconsin, Indiana and Tennessee. He is still studying at the Cosmopolitan School in Chicago, from the two Rosenwald awards, which include voice, piano, harmony, history, theory and dramatic art. Added to his native genius, is a convincing, magnetic personality, which is winning for him, the admiration of many friends among all races.

One listens to John Greene with the strong conviction that the Singer and his songs play no uncertain part toward spiritual attainment to high art, in the musical life of our American Nation.

# UNPUBLISHED WORKS: POEMS
## *c. 1900–c. 1942*

❧ ❧ ❧

*A long standing interest in the Bahai faith (expressed in numerous spiritual allusions) and the importance of family are exemplified in Bush-Banks's unpublished poems. She continued to produce poetry until a few years before her death.*

*In addition to the poems presented in this section, four others can be found in Chapters 4, 6, and 8 of Bush-Banks's unpublished memoirs,* The Lure of the Distances, *which appears later in this volume. The four poems are "The Great Adventure" (Ch. 4), "The Magdalene" (Ch. 6), "Roses" (Ch. 6), and one untitled poem (Ch. 8). Fragments and variants of other poems, both published and unpublished, also appear in the memoirs.*

# SYMBOLS

Time was when holly, evergreen
　　And bright red berry,
Were holy, age-old tokens,
　　Of abundant yule-tide cheer.
When carols echoed and re-echoed
　　The immortal message
Of "peace on earth," good-will,
　　To all mankind.

And now, these precious symbols,
　　Are shorn of sacred meaning,
They are but feeble gestures
　　Revealing man's descent
From lofty faith and purpose
　　From love to brother-man,
To unholy planes of selfishness,
　　And worthless gain.

# TO THE MEMORY OF HARRIET
# BEECHER STOWE

Across the troubled years
　　Of strife and conflict,
Comes the clear echo
　　Of a stirring soul-cry
That would not hold its peace.

A Nation listens,
　　And recalls the dauntless courage
Of a gentle patriot
　　Who, with pen of love and pity

Wrote the wrongs of Human Bondage
  And its cruel sway.

Unceasing in her plea
  That "Right must triumph over wrong"
She dared to cry aloud
  Against a Nation's shame:

With overwhelming love
  For helpless fellow-men,
She could not be content
  Until their chafing fetters
Were unbound.

O fine desire! O matchless love,
  May we in fadeless memory
Keep ever burning
  On the altars of our souls
The fragrant incense
  Of unfailing loyalty.

## CHALLENGE

What did you say, Comrade?
You're going to lie down—you're through—
Why, what's happening to you?
It can't be that you flinch
From the maddening roar
Of life's shrapnel and shell,
Or even the sickening sight of gore,
You've seen and heard it all before.

Your body's frail?
Yes, but you've carried a light
That will not fail,

And, with ringing laughter.
Defied the fears
That lurked in all the tragic years.

When you said,
"I'll stand and see others pass by"
Did you note the baffled look
In the eyes of Youth?
Did you hear the haunting cry:
"Well, if you're beaten, so am I"?

Why, we haven't heard the last command
"Stack arms!"
So, comrade, have done
With these false alarms,
O No! you're not through,
And you won[']t lie down,—
That's the way cowards die,
Not you and I!

# VISION *

### 1.

Easter dawned, but I was weary
    With the fever and the pain,
And my very soul seemed sinking
    Never to revive again.

### 2.

And as thus I lay, in weakness
    Tossing, restless in my pain,
Softly in my room came stealing
    One triumphant, glad, sweet strain.

*"An Easter Echo" in *Memories of Calvary*.

3.

Sung by little children's voices
   From God's Temple o'er the way,
Sung in faith and full believing;
   O'er my soul, those words hold sway,—

4.

"He is risen! He is risen!
   Wipe away the falling tear.
Sin and pain and Death are vanquished!
   For the Lord Christ draweth near."

5.

Hushed at once was my complaining,
   And my earthly sight grew dim,
For my soul had caught a vision,
   And, rejoicing, cried to Him,—

6.

O, my resurrected Savior!
   O, thou Conqueror of strife!
May I hold fast to thy promise,
   Let it echo thro' my life,—

7.

Till I sing in Death triumphant,—
   "Wipe away the falling tear
He is risen! He is risen!
   Lo, the Lord Christ draweth near!"

# BONDAGE
## A Tribute to Colored Motherhood

Up through the ruthless sacrilege
Of outraged motherhood,
   These women came,

With bodies scarred,
With anguished souls.

Still upward—with undaunted faith
To do and dare
   Expanding into glowing
Womanhood.

To-day, these matchless women rise
In peerless- dusk-brown beauty,
   Destined to be
A priceless Heritage
To their children
   Of to-morrow.


## FILLED WITH YOU


By your fireside, close to my side,
You are sitting silently,
Eyes so tender—I surrender
To their charm and mystery:
   All the room is filled with you.

Tho' no word of hope you've spoken,
Still my faith remains unbroken:
All the room is filled with you, dear,
   Filled with you.

In the twilight, by your firelight,
I would linger yet awhile,
Waiting gladly, loving madly
You, your sweetness and your smile:
   All my world is filled with you.

Even tho' your love lies sleeping,
In the silence you are keeping:

All my world is filled with you, dear,
  Filled with you.

# HARLEM

Where the language of the tropics,
  And sea-girt isles
Is heard above the mellow tones
  Of Dixie's sons and daughters.

Where magic midnight,
  Weaves its subtle spell,
O'er all the denizens
  Within this realm of merry madness.

Harlem—colorful Harlem,
With its ideals and its longing,
  With its love of Life and laughter,
Harlem, the mystic Highway of Manhattan.

# LOVE'S LAMENT

Ah, love, if you could only know
  The longing in this heart of mine,
You would unsay those fateful words,
  And I no longer would repine.

Your fond desire is to share
  All that you have—all that you own,
I ask of you far greater wealth,
  The priceless gift of love, alone.

Steadfast and true I still remain,
  In spite of utter loneliness,
O, let thy soul go forth with mine,
  Upon this quest of happiness.

For love is life, and life is love,
  Break not the bond 'twixt thee and me,
Then shall this precious, priceless gift,
  Be ours for all eternity.


# DOGGEREL

## Marie Buries a Little Bird

I buried a bird beneath a tree
  Because it touched the heart of me.
That he had met a tragic end.——
  And so, I thought I'd be his friend.

## Jimmy (Italian Friend)

I know someone not far away
  Who has a pleasant smile,——
His name is Jimmy, and he helps
  To make this life worth while.

He knows just how to greet a friend
  His heart is brave and true;
So, keep on smiling while I send
  My kindest thoughts to you.


# CATAWBA*

O memory,
  Again I wander thru the realm

* A variant fragment of this poem appears in Chapter 3 of *The Lure of the Distances*.

Of unforgotten days,
I tread upon the down softness
Of a lane of leaves,
Where the scent of pine-trees lingers.

And now walled in
By God's great hills, I tarry
With the kindly mountaineers,
Around a blazing fire-place,
And listen to an old man, reminiscent.
While pattering rain-drops make music,
On the slanting roof.

The fire-light dims,
And then comes peaceful slumber
Within a white-washed room,
Until the sun of morn,
Gleams thru the weather-beaten logs:
O memory!
O realm of unforgotten days!

# THE KEEPERS OF THE HOUSE
## (in memory of Eugene Debs)

Art thou alarmed,
O Troubled Dwellers in the House of Life,
That in this hour,
The Cosmic mutterings of Coming Wars,
And Wrongs in Labor's Name,
Are heard above the Human Cry
    'Gainst Inhumanity?

Discard thy fears,
And rouse thee to the Pulsing Call

Of those, who, undismayed,
Keep ceaseless vigilance
E'en at the Portals,
Where their voices blend full mightily,
While hurling forth
　　The Challenge of the Just.

They spurn defeat,
Nor shrink from Prison Walls,
Or threats of Death;
Urged on by Holy Purpose to destroy
Age-old foundations,
Laid in strong contempt
Of Just Demand
　　In Common Brotherhood.

Rise then, in faith,
O Troubled Dwellers in the House of Life,
And by such faith,
Uphold these Comrades All,
Who, in Our Day,
Are opening Doors of Hope.
Fear not! the Keepers of the House,
　　Have rightly willed it so.

## THE TEMPLE GLORIOUS

With souls aflame
'Neath the sun-lit canopy of blue
We stood that glorious morn
　　On the hallowed soil
　　Of the temple that is to be:
　　　　Children of many nations
　　　　Kindred offspring of the All-Divine.

We caught a vision rare
Of pilgrims, faring forth from many lands,
   O'er the hopeful trail
   Of waiting years,
To the wide-flung gates
   Of the temple that is to be.

Keeping their Quest Divine
   With faces radiant—with hearts attuned
To the Call of the Infinite One
   Chanting the strain Triumphant
"Onward we move in the Holy strength
   Of the ONENESS OF MANKIND:
   The gray dawn breaks—behold!
     This is The Day of God."


## TRAILS

Mist—and the dim outline
Of winding ways,
   Lead on, Life!

I pay no heed to surging winds
Amid the cypress' shade,
Or mournful lyrics
   Of the weeping-willow tree.

Lead on! past tangled weed
And stubborn brush,
Where human fears, like monsters
   Lie in ambush.

Still onward to the open,
Where I envision

The Horizon of the heights,
    Life, lead on!


# WHITHER?*

O venturous soul,
    I know that thou has kept
Thy wing-ed way
    Across the centuries,
Oft pausing for a swift descent,
    Whenever a kindred cry
Has filtered thro' the ether:
    For thou art full-attuned
To human yearnings.

On, on thro' aeons,
    Wilt thou fly,
Immortal one?
    Upward and beyond
The cosmic realm,
    E'en to the heights
Divinely rarefied,
    And wilt thou tarry there?

Or, surcharged
    With the love of God,
Wilt thou descend again,
    And yet again,
To breathe an ancient blessing,
    On waiting humankind?

*A variant fragment of this poem appears in Chapter 6, *The Lure of the Distances*.

## ECHOES
(an interpretation of the origin of Negro
Spirituals)

Fair fields of whiteness,
'Neath sun-bright skies of blue:
Dark forms, moving, bending
All the day long,
Amid the wondrous whiteness:
Rich, mellow voices,
Singing strange, rare bits of song,
That seem to laugh, and sigh, and moan,
While hands, dark, toil-trained hands,
Pile up the snowy cotton,
For a waiting mart.

Toil-days, and song-days,
Merging into years of hopeful waiting,
For free days and glad days,
While the strange, rare bits of song,
That seem to laugh, and sigh, and moan,
Grow into richer, sweeter harmonies,
Until are born
The lyrics of a nation.

## ART?

Is it a riot of color on canvas
  With reckless dashes of red-gold
'Gainst a vivid sunset sky?
A sea-gull on the wing,
  A lone pine-tree on a snow-white mountain-side?

Or a poet's dream of day-dawn,
Soothing twilight,
   And the love-laden light of the moon?

Is it Venus or winged Victory,
   Wrought in bronze clay?
Or the witching light in a woman's eye,
   Wooing her mate?
Or the insistent love-call
   Of her seductive smile?

When a comrade pours out living joy,
   Into the depths of a lonely heart,
Or brings a smile to a joyless face,
   Is it Art, divine?
Is Art, Life,
   Is Life the Art of Arts?


# FLIGHT

A butterfly alights
On a bright green hedge,
Sways with grace
On its very edge:
Like an airy spectre it seems to cling,
Then, off again upon the wing.

Ah, Love, is yours
The same wily art,
Poised with grace
On the edge of my heart,
Just for a moment there to cling,
Then off again upon the wing?

# FRUITION
## (to Marie)

A little brown face—a long silken curl
 Tied with a ribbon of blue,
A look of wonder in soft, brown eyes
 With the love-light shining thru'.

Ah! the vision is stamped indelibly,
 Sweetly clear in my memory now;
I remember the smile on the little brown face
 I remember the childish "vow."

O, the comfort and cheer it gave that day
 And the spoken words rang true,—
"Don't worry, for I will soon grow up
 And I'll be a help to you."

A help? why you've been far more than that,
 You are making Life easy and bright,
Peace flows within, the gloom has passed,
 And, at "even-tide"—it's "light."

A little brown face—a long silken curl
 Tied with a ribbon of blue,
And the childish "vow" has been faithfully kept
 And the love-light still shines thru'.

From Mama
July 13, 1935

# HONEY-SWEET
## (to Helen)

Twenty years ago to-day,
 In the fragrant month of roses,

A little baby girl came our way,
　　To prove the love that God discloses;
Precious gift! from head to feet,
　　And we called her "Honey-sweet."

Now on this, her natal day,
　　In the lovely month of June,
With enduring love we say—
　　"That we find our hearts in tune
To the song of joy, replete
　　With our love for 'Honey-sweet.' "

And through all her golden youth,
　　She has been our dearest treasure;
Brought to us in very truth,
　　Years of unalloyed pleasure;
O, Life could not be complete
　　Had we not our "Honey-sweet."

Best of all, O "Honey-sweet,"
　　To the Master you've been true,
You can never know defeat,
　　For He watches over you,
And, with Him, we now repeat—
　　"How we love you, 'Honey-sweet.' "
　　　　　　From your
　　　　　　　　"Sweetheart Grandma."
　　　　　　　　　June 27, 1935


# MOONLIGHT


The radiant searchlight
　　Of the heavens,
Sends down her glowing whiteness,
　　Where darkened streets,

And haunts of living things
Enfold themselves
Within her mantle.

Stars, countless stars,
Soften(?) the dais of crystal,
Like bits of crystal,
Soft-bedded in the azure blue,
Veil their brightness,
Paying gracious tribute
To the Enchantress
Of the night-sky.


## OASIS (FRIENDSHIP)

Red sunrise,
After gray daydawn:
Shade-trees, limpid pools,
Apart from burning noon-tide:
Gold and carmine, blending
Into purple twilight:
Moonlight,
Caressing silent stars.

You, heart's-ease
Urging me forward,
Leading me onward
To the hopeful distances,
While the mist clears,
On the far horizon.

# SCARS

Sometimes our souls
Are seared so deep
By penetrating wounds
Of cruel words,
That pierce us to the quick,
Until, as years pass on,
We are no longer shocked
By this recurrence,
Nor recoil in sad surprise.

The scars remain
But all the pain and sting
Have been removed
By God's good grace;
In tender mercy
He dulls our sense of memory,
And helps us to forget.

# SHADOWS:
## Dedicated to Miss Marian Anderson*

## Prologue

Nolanda, the African maiden, does the jungle dance and is
conscious of the wild ecstasy of jungle rhythm. Later, the
urgent primal call within her seems to forecast the centuries
of bondage under the pitiless white light of advanced civili-

*See chapter 5 in *The Lure of the Distances*, for background information
concerning this poem.

zation, to be fraught with untold suffering for her people, who, in spite of SHADOWS, attain to great heights.

Nolanda follows Life into the shaded places, seeking to know their mystic meanings. Life assures her that what she sees and hears are only SHADOWS from the realm of rich African attainment.

> Life called insistently—,
> "Come, leave the glare
> Of sun-lighted highways,
> Come where hidden recesses
> Give pause and understand."

> I followed Life
> Into the shaded place,
> And listened—
> Ravishing notes of song,
> Lilted their wing-ed way,
> Into the very heart of me:
> Words, rich-toned words,
> Laid bare the burning dramas
> Of the soul.

> I looked into faces,
> Smooth ebony, golden-tinted brown,
> Pale yellows:
> Into eyes, glowing with steady light
> From the altar-fires
> Of age-old yearnings.

> "O Life," I cried,
> "O subtle interpreter
> Of unknown destinies,
> Unfold the mystic meaning
> Of these shaded places."

Life made answer,
"These are not mysteries:
Smooth ebony, golden-tinted brown, pale yellows,
Are the inheritors
Of ancient Art-Realms;
Haunting harmonies, burning words,
Are only forecasts
Of things that be."

In these verses, I have attempted to interpret our inheri-
nces from an early African civilization[.]

# AN "R.N.'S" SOLILOQUY*
## (with apologies to Shakespeare)

To eat or not to eat: that is the question:
Would it be best to load the dinner-tray
With tempting viands—pile on pile,
Consume them—and, full soon, go forth
Unto my nightly quarters, with ripe red fruit
Thrust deeply in the bulging pockets
Of an R.N.'s gown?
To eat again—and then—to sleep,
To sleep—ah yes—to dream
Of coming morns, when, with everhastening feet
I fare me forth again upon the noble? quest
Of food—much food—more food,
To be devoured, even at the risk
Of growing corpulency?

* This poem was probably written for Bush-Banks's daughter, Marie Bush
Horton, who was one of New York City's first African-American registered
nurses.

To eat or not to eat; Aye! there's the rub;
To suffer all the slings and arrows
Of ravenous desire,
Or, by the eating act,—oppose them?
To know full well
That Staten Island's healthful breeze
Doth add more pounds
To the "Voracious One"?
And yet, should I refrain from this new found delight
Ah me! "it would break my heart"
"Twould break my heart."
Perchance by some uncanny Art
Or magic mystery, one could eat and eat and eat
And still possess a sylph-like form
Petite and slender.


## ASHES OF INCENSE

A tiny jar of burnished clay,
And the lingering scent
Of fragrant, fire-spent ashes,
Ashes, recalling vibrant life,
From a distant Orient,
Or exotic clime.

A quiet hour,
And the clinging memory
Of friends, unseen,
Still vibrant,
With the comradeship
Of other days, and years to come,
Untold—eternal.

## JUST GOD AND I

Sometimes I shut the door on all the world
And go alone to that most secret place
Where there is only God—
Just God and I, then
Together we go over subtle acts
Mistakes, and small hypocrisies of mine,
I strip myself from shame, from shackles free,
And stand aghast at my duplicity.

We look, just God and I, into my heart,
And tho' I shrink, we gaze there to the depth;
And though I tremble, shamed by what we find
I suffer, too, a kind of painful joy . . .

And while I often find it hard to bear
The burning of God's knowing eyes on me
I feel me stronger grown, just from their gaze;
My nakedness, it seems to me, is clothed
In rainment new that is most wondrous fair,
When next I venture forth, I wear
Sincerity, the gift that God in secret gave to me.

## BARTHE
(a brown sculptor, after viewing the bust of his
"Tortured Negro")

O eyes of youth,
From out those yearning depths,
What seest thou?
Dost vision souls

A'tremble with desire
To break the bonds of flesh,
And woo the Sculptor's magic touch,
Living anew—immortalized
    In bronze?

O deft, sure hands,
Full eager to create,
Dream visions of centuries gone by,
Tone-masters, heroes,
And lamented bard?
Or the tortured visage
Of thine own blood and kind,
Writhing, helpless,
In Freedom's galling bonds?
    What shapest thou?

# LEE

Eyes of wonder, soul aflame,
With eager yearning
To fathom the unfathomed

Scanning the heights with high desire,
To solve the mystery
Of Life's subtle meanings.

Ever searching, ever athirst
For clearer concepts
Of the realms unknown.

Never-ending is the quest,
    Ever and always
The eternal question Why?

# THRILLS

Isn't life liveable,
Gloom unforgivable,
In the green of the spring-time,
The rose-blush of summer,
The red and gold of the autumn,
And the white whiteness of winter?
   Isn't life liveable?

# DOING OUR BIT
## Nov. 4, 1942

Our soldier boys are far from home
Obeying their Country's call;
And we must offer fervent prayers
That God will protect them all.

And we can give them courage, too
By writing words of cheer,
That they may know our faith in them
Is lasting and sincere.

And while they strive so loyally
Our freedom to defend,
May we every pray for their safe return,
When War and strife shall end.

# "KEEP ON, KEEPING ON"
## A Tribute

To the Late Richard B. Harrison, ("de Lawd" in *Green Pastures,*) whose favorite saying was "Keep on, keeping on["]

A Grand Old Sage from the House of Art,
  Just "kept on keeping on"
While hope flamed red in his royal heart;
  He made the goal—he won.

O the way was'n[']t always smooth and bright,
  There were paths where no "footlights" gleamed:
But he "walked by faith" and not "by sight";
  Just plodded along—and dreamed—

That he'd surely reach the longed-sought place,
  Where there'd be no "darkened scene";
He would not pause—he would keep up the pace,
  And he'd find those "pastures green."

He did—and lo! at the end of the road,
  Rich reward awaited him there;
The "footlights gleamed" and the "droplights glowed,"
There were "sidelights" everywhere.

And thousands cheered as he played his "role"
  With dignity and grace;
While the light of laughter in his soul
  Beamed from his radiant face.

Then the "curtain fell" but it wasn't the end.
  For his "act" still holds the stage,
And the flaming fires of hope ascend
  From the heart of the "Grand Old Sage"—

Upward to those who dare to aspire
  To the goal which he has won,
And they'll surely reach their "high desire."
  If they "Keep on keeping on."

# UNPUBLISHED WORKS: PLAYS, VIGNETTES, ESSAYS, SKETCHES

## *C. 1917–C. 1941*

๛ ๛ ๛

*Bush-Banks's prose works reveal the evolution of her social and political consciousness. The end of World War I, the Negro Renaissance, and the Great Depression seem to have particularly affected her, and in tone and ouput, her production during the interwar years proved stimulating and fruitful. Among friends and associates from younger generations or divergent backgrounds, she was able to reaffirm her focus on black pride and the humanitarian ethos; her earlier familiarity with socialism kept her in step with an increased awareness of communism, and her interest in the Bahai faith became further developed as well.*

*The results of these influences on Bush-Banks reflect what critics of African-American literature have noted—that, in general, black compositions from this era exhibit a spirit of faith, ethnic pride, optimism, and resiliency that is lacking in literature from the majority community.*

*Bush-Banks's plays and dramatic fragments have varied settings, but all share a message of compassion, empathy, and faith in humankind. Many of the plays were written for children or youths at her School of Expression in Chicago, or for Sunday school participants in New York. In these dramas, Bush-Banks guided the young through what she referred to as "behavior drama," which appears to be the combination of a creative and didactic experience.*

*Although apparently not published,* Indian Trails; or, Trail of the Montauk *was performed, combining didacticism with a kind of historical propaganda.*

*Other monologues and oral presentations show more adult tastes in themes that address the effects of war, as in* The Awakening: A Prophecy, *or that present social satire mixed with self-effacement, as in "Greenwich Village Highlights," or that celebrate negritude, as in "Shadows: Dedicated to Miss Marian Anderson" (in previous section). These short pieces could have been produced in Bush-Banks's art studios in Chicago and New York.*

*As shown earlier, several of Bush-Banks's essays found their way into print. One that did not—the visceral "What About Our Loyal Colored Americans?"—is suitable for a letter to an editor, an address to a rally, or an opinion column. This extraordinary polemic must have been instigated by the December 7, 1941, attack on Pearl Harbor. It is a definite departure from her general admiration of oriental culture.*

*The vignettes, "New Year Musings" and "Black Com-*

munism," underscore Bush-Banks's Christian spirit and New England value system. It is unclear whether she wrote them for publication or as a private commentary. On the other hand, she submitted several of the Aunt Viney's Sketches for publication and for possible radio broadcast (see Appendix). In form, content, and characterization, these sketches are an outstanding contribution to African-American letters. They are prefaced in this volume by Bush-Banks's introduction.

# THE AWAKENING—A PROPHECY

SCENE—*The Desert of Desire*

11

## CHARACTERS

THE YEARNING O—*O. W. Bush-Banks*
SPIRIT OF LOVE—*Lee Rapoport*

*(The Yearning One approaches—Soliloquy)*

YEARNING ONE:   The gray dawn is breaking, and I must journey onward o'er the trackless waste of shifting sands, surrounded by this dead silence, in search of peace—which to me, seems almost unattainable. I have journeyed thro' many lands, amid confusion and cruel strife, the sound of which still lingers in my ears. Unbroken shadows cast their endless length o'er all the troubled earth. Waves of unutterable loneliness overwhelm me.

SPIRIT OF LOVE:   *(unseen)* Mortal! Thou art not alone.

YEARNING ONE:   Not alone! Can it be that from out this dead stillness, I hear the welcome sound of a voice other than my own? Speak once again, wh'ere thou art!

SPIRIT OF LOVE:   Most gladly will I grant thy earnest request. I am known as the Spirit of Love.

YEARNING ONE:   And thy mission?

SPIRIT OF LOVE:    To find and enlighten all who are despairing on the Desert of Desire.

YEARNING ONE:    Can this be true?

SPIRIT OF LOVE:    Aye, it is true indeed, if thou desirest. I will draw near to thee *(approaches)*. Now canst thou believe?

YEARNING ONE:    O Spirit of Love, I can no longer deny thy presence, which is so needful in my hour of fear and dismay.

SPIRIT OF LOVE:    What are they fears, and why art thou dismayed?

YEARNING ONE:    Spirit of Love, I am fearful for myself and all humanity, as we pass th thro' these stark tragedies of Life. I am dismayed, when I behold the horrors of this Age, and I find no refuge from them. Surely thou, too, art conscious of this World Catastrophe—the cruel slaughter of innocent children—men and women's hearts failing them for fear. It is all so helpless—canst thou not perceive that great dangers, and even death await us?

SPIRIT OF LOVE:    O Yearning One, I can indeed, and I have known all thro' the Ages that many wise ones have foretold the coming this coming of this day.

YEARNING ONE:    And why have mortals failed to listen to these age-old warnings?

SPIRIT OF LOVE:    Because their desire for World Control, greed and gain at any cost, have dwarfed their best impulses and robbed them of the joy of Brotherhood.

YEARNING ONE:    Spirit of Love, if this be true, when shall this bitter struggle cease [?] If the prophecy of Ages has failed to enlighten them, what power can restrain them?

SPIRIT OF LOVE:    The awakened power of love within everyman's soul, which is divine in its source and will bring forth everlasting peace.

YEARNING ONE: But what of all the suffering and bloodshed? What part do they play in the coming of peace?

SPIRIT OF LOVE: These are the death-throes of an old order of Life. Man is slowly but surely becoming surfeited with the uselessness of human warfare. Already he is beginning to yearn for a New Order of living when only love will flow from Man to Brother-Man.

YEARNING ONE: Tell me, O Spirit of Love, hast thou a clear vision of the time that is to be?

SPIRIT OF LOVE: I have, O Yearning One. Man will yet experience the rich value of unified purpose, rare attainments in Art and Industry, and, best of all, a deep, inner peace, when each shall be for all and all for each.

YEARNING ONE: Dear Spirit of Love, thou hast inspired me. The shadows are lifting, and the Desert of Desire glows with the radiant light of hope. I can now move forward, undisturbed by fear and dismay.

SPIRIT OF LOVE: Come then, and together we shall keep this fadeless vision of the World that is to be.

EXIT

(Most gladly will I go with thee, for now I know that Love can never fail.)

# PAGEANT—THE MARCH OF TIME—A PROPHESY

## CHARACTERS

| | |
|---|---|
| Narrator | Liberty |
| Time | Good-will |
| Wisdom—*with two others* | Art |
| Peace | Music |
| Love | Drama |

## PROLOGUE *(with music)*

**Narrator:** To-day, over all the troubled earth, we hear the discordant sounds of tumult and confusion, strife and conflict. A sense of unutterable weariness broods over the children of men, filling them with infinite longings for the coming of a new world order, when peace and harmony shall ultimately reign.

Amid this direful chaos, Time—the relentless interpreter of Life and destinies, moves steadily forward—never pausing—leaving in its trail, despairing humanity, with its crushing weight of misery and woe.

**Wisdom** *(soft music, impressive and decisive)*

**Narrator:** But, throughout the ages, Hope has ever been man's guiding-star, and we dare to dream or catch a vision

184

of the new day, when Wisdom, gleaning her knowledge from the book of Books, shall reveal to the waiting world, the wise and holy purpose of a divine Creator, to banish all darkness, and bring forth a clear, glowing dawn.

## PEACE *(soft music)*

NARRATOR:  Then, the long-sought Peace, like the wings of a dove, shall hover gently over the earth, causing strife and conflict to cease, dispelling all fear, and encircling all nations and people within the bonds of never-ending unity.

## LOVE *(soft music)*

NARRATOR:  And Love shall appear with outstretched hands, beckoning her fellow-beings to a nobler life, where each shall be for all and all for each. Where the forces of evil can no longer prevail, nor sever one link from the golden chain of loving kindness.

## LIBERTY *(martial music)*

NARRATOR:  Liberty shall come forth, holding high her torch of light, proclaiming to all people, their sacred right to live, unmolested by injustice, intolerance and cruelty. Rather shall all humanity build a lasting foundation for freedom of thought and righteous living.

## GOOD-WILL *(soft music)*

NARRATOR:  And Good-will shall appear in the spirit of true comradeship, bringing to the children of earth—faith and courage—to seek a definite purpose in life, to use their talents, and to attain to the highest possible standards of accomplishment.

## ART *(soft music)*

NARRATOR:   And Art shall paint in glowing colors, rare scenes from real life, nature [and] human experience, because Wisdom, and all the finer attributes have revealed to man's soul, a deeper sense of beauty and its priceless contribution to a new humanity.

## MUSIC *(varying tones)*

NARRATOR:   Music, in all its sweetness, shall be recognized, as a divine influence, its tender, soothing, triumphant strains, shall inspire men to loftier desires, interpreting the complex meanings of life, unfolding rare genius, and enriching the lives and motives of all who discern its fine attainment.

## DRAMA *(soft, very emotional)*

NARRATOR:   Drama shall reach the highest plane of human expression. It shall play its colorful part in revealing hidden depths of emotion. It shall enact thrilling scenes from real life in all of its phases. It shall unfold the beauty of man's soul, and endow humanity with a new consciousness of the joy of living.

# SEQUENCE

*(Time and the other characters move across the stage to the strains of a stirring march, while the Narrator speaks, as follows)*

NARRATOR *(triumphant music)*: And now, amid the uncertainty of to-day, Time and the Chosen Ones of our dream-vision still move steadily onward. Thus, do they pass, with an enduring hope for the fulfillment of prophesy, in the world that is to be. . . .

FINIS

# INDIAN TRAILS:
## OR, TRAIL OF THE MONTAUK*

SCENE:    *Tepee of the Montauks*

ACT 1.    *Prophesy of Wan-to-co-no-mese; O-Ne-Ne departs.*
ACT 2.    *Pongomo and Appanch quarrel. Quashawan returns.*
ACT 3.    *Return of O-Ne-Ne.*

## CAST

WAN-TO-CO-NO-MESE: *Montauk's Wise Man, Abuki*
BIG CHIEF HIGH HORSE
PONGOMO: *Fiery Young Brave, Shenoka's lover*
O-NE-NE: *Wild Pigeon—who is sent to Great White Father*
ME-TOW-AH: *Leader of Maiden's dance*
SHE-NO-KA: *Pongomo's sweetheart*
APPANCH: *Friendly Shinnecock*
QUASHAWAN: *Montauk's Wise Woman*
WE-NO-NAH: *Who suggests Joy Dance*
FLASHING SUNLIGHT: *Indian Maiden*
DAWN-OF-DAY
STAR OF EVENING
SILVER MOONBEAM: *Squaw*
FADING TWILIGHT
MO-RE-AH
FLEET-OF-FOOT: *Arrow-maker*

*Only Act 1, Scene 1, and Act 3, Scene 2, are extant.

SEQUANAH: *Maker of bowls and backboards*
SASSAKATOW: *Medicine-man*

*Act 1.*—Wan-to-co-no-mese prophesies. Maidens are driven from teepee by Pale-faces. The Indian's Lament to Wa-kan-da is heard. O-Ne-Ne is chosen to visit the Great White Father, to plead for restoration of Montauk lands.

*Act 2.*—The squaws and maidens are lon[e]ly, after the departure of O-ne-ne, and seek to make merry with the Dance of the Indian Maidens. A quarrel starts between Pongomo and a friendly Shinnecock Indian, because, Pongomo is jealous of She-no-ka, a beautiful Montauk maiden. Quashawan, Montauk's Wish Woman, returns to Montauk in time to stop the dispute. The dance goes on.

*Act 3.*—O-ne-ne returns, bringing good news from the Great White Father . . . He also brings gifts and trophies from friendly tribes whom he has met on his journey. He finally introduces, Starlight, a beautiful Mohawk maiden, as his sweetheart. Montauks become angry but finally receive her graciously. O-ne-ne reads the answer of the Great White Father, who has restored Montauk lands. There is great rejoicing. They chant the Tribal Vow of Victory, and dance joyously.

# SYNOPSIS

The lands of the Montauk Indians have been taken by the Pale-faces and the tribe has sent O-Ne-Ne, their chief, to the Great White Father to intercede for them. During O-Ne-Ne's absence, a number of events take place, among them, the return of Quashawan, Montauk's Wise Woman. O-Ne-Ne finally returns bringing tidings that the Great White Father has restored their land to them.

# SCENES FROM *THE TRAIL OF THE MONTAUK*

## ACT I, SCENE I.

WANTOCONOMESE: Quashawan, our Wise Woman, returns once more to the land of her fathers. Welcome O Quashawan!

QUASHAWAN: After many moons, after many moons, O my people, Quashawan comes again to the teepees of our fathers. You have seen the snows of many winters, and the blue skies of many summers, since Quashawan last sojourned with you. The passing years have wrought many changes with the Montauks. Tell me, O Wantoconomese, do my people live in safety and comfort?

WANTOCONOMESE: Wantoconomese will speak the truth to Quashawan. His heart is heavy. The trail along the teepees is thick with the footprints of the palefaces. Ere the rising of another moon, trouble comes to Montauk!

SASSAKATOW: Ugh' Wantoconomese is old and full of years and his words are but the foolish babblings of a senseless papoose. My people need not fear. See! Sassakatow, has many arrows, many arrows to protect our people! The soil of Montauk shall run crimson with the blood of the palefaces. Sassakatow is keen and cunning. He will slay them! Pay no heed to Wantoconomese—his days of warfare are over—Ha!

QUASHAWAN: Shame on you, Sassakatow, why do ye laugh when Wantoconomese speaks—why do ye say that his ears are old and that he cannot hear—long, long before Sassakatow was—Wantoconomese was—has spoken words of wisdom. Hear him!

WANTOCONOMESE: Wantoconomese cares not for the idle

words of Sassakatow. Youth knows not what it speaks—hot blood runs through his veins. Wantoconomese has seen the risings and settings of many suns. The waning of many moons. Behold! Even now in the distance, comes Shenoka, Montauk's favorite daughter, fleeing to the wigwam of Wantoconomese. Said I not true, and the moon is not yet risen! Shenoka, why come ye here, fleeing like the startled Red Deer,? Is not this the land of your fathers? What terror has come upon you?

SHE-NO-KA: O Wantoconomese, and my people, the teepees of our fathers are no longer safe for the maidens of Montauk. We were dancing gaily upon the green grass, when suddenly the pale-faces came upon us, crying "Get you gone from here—this is no longer the land of the Redskin—we have made it the white man's country." For this reason, O Quashawan and my people, I have fled to the wigwam of Wantoconomese.

QUASHAWAN: O my people, the shadow of coming days, falls fast upon us. Who shall lead the Tribe back to its own? Who shall contend for Montauk? What say you, Wantoconomese?

*(The Lament, chanted by Wantoconomese)*

O Wakanda! Wakanda! hear thou the cry of thy children,
Make light the heart of the Red Man!
Gone are our lands and our homes, gone are our Braves
    and our warriors:
Our wigwam fires are but ashes, our councils and chiefs
    are no more.
The wild winds sweep over our dead, and the sighing of
    Autumn leaves.
Is heard thro' the desolate forest.
We are despised and distressed
Neath the pitiless hand of the pale-face.

Soften the heart of the white man!
Restore Montauk to its own—O Wakanda! Wakanda!

(CURTAIN)

# SCENES FROM *THE TRAIL OF THE MONTAUK*

## ACT III    SCENE II

QUASHAWAN:    The sun of noon beams brightly, O my people and the heart of Quashawan is glad and so shall yours be, for O-ne-ne, our Wild Pigeon returns to-day after his long trail to the Pale-faces, and it may be that he will bring good news for Montauk. But where is the maiden, She-no-ka, and the Young Brave, Appanch, son of a great Shinnecock, a kindred of our people? Mo-re-ah, thine eye is keen and clear as the eagle, seest thou them in the distance?

MO-RE-AH:    Aye, they come, Quashawan, but Appanch does not seem well pleased with the maiden, She-no-ka.

QUASHAWAN:    How now! Appanch, thy face is like the storm-cloud, ere it breaks in fury over the distant hills—is this thine only greeting to Quashawan? Thy welcome to her home-coming? Quashawan bids Appanch speak if aught is troubling him?

APPANCH:    The maiden She-no-ka, is untrue to Appanch. Three times have I trailed her to the Wigwam of a stranger. Appanch likes it not—Appanch will kill him! *(draws knife— Quashawan interposes.)*

QUASHAWAN:    Cease thine anger, Appanch, thy rash words are like a consuming fire, and can avail thee nothing. Quashawan would ask the royal son of a great Shinnecock "Shall the Red Man slay his brother?" It may be that he rears his wigwam here in peace and friendship. Let the maiden She-no-ka speak!

SHE-NO-KA: She-no-ka is a true daughter of Montauk, and scorns to seek the Lodge of a stranger. She-no-ka, saw that he needed food and drink, and with her own hands, she placed them at the doorway of his Wigwam. The young Brave told Sh-no-ka, that he is Canonchet, the son of a mighty Narragansett, and he rears his wigwam here in Peace and Friendship, that he might be near our people. She-no-ka's heart is true to Appanch. So speaks the Montauk maiden.

QUASHAWAN: She-no-ka's words are pleasing to Quashawan and her speech rings true. My people need not fear the Narragansett. He will bring no harm upon us. He comes from the Great Algonquin, a mighty tribe of Red Men. See! He gives the sign of peace—has the anger of Appanch passed?

APPANCH: Appanch is ashamed of himself, and he asks the maiden She-no-ka and the Narragansett to forgive him. Appanch heap much loves She-no-ka.

SHE-NO-KA: Appanch, there is Peace between us.

QUASHAWAN: 'Tis well that She-no-ka and our young Brave forget their anger—Come! Rise! my people, O-ne-ne comes in the distance! Welcome! O-ne-ne, do you bring good tidings to Montauk?

O-NE-NE: At last my people, O-ne-ne brings papers from the White Chief of the Nation, declaring that our lands have been returned to us, and Montauk comes into its own.

QUASHAWAN: Rejoice, O my people,—let the Tribal Vow ring through the forest—O-ne-ne our wild Pigeon shall lead us!

### The Tribal Vow

The Light has come! The Light has come!
And Wa-kan-da bids up hope!
Let the pale-face listen to the Red Man's vow—

While our father's blood runs thro' our veins,
We will not yield our right,
Tho the Trail of Montauk be crimson with woe;
We will hold to our fathers' lands,
Till our Tribe is scattered to the winds of Heaven
Till the Setting Sun shall be no more!
The Light! The Light shall be no more!

(CURTAIN)

# THE DEPARTURE OF NAOMI AND RUTH*

## CHARACTERS

NAOMI    RUTH    ORPAH    MIRIAM
ESTHER    RACHEL    LE'AH    VASHTI

SCENE 1. *The home of Miriam, in a village of the land of Moab*

SCENE 2. *Naomi starts on her journey to Bethlehem*

In Scene 1, Miriam, Esther and Rachel are sewing on garments for the needy ones of the village. They await the coming of Le'ah and Vashti, who bring them tidings of the beloved widow, Naomi, whom, they learn, is preparing to return to Bethlehem, the land of her nativity. They are deeply touched, and saddened by this unexpected news.

In Scene 2, Naomi journeys forth at daybreak, on her way to Bethlehem, followed by her two daughters-in-law, Ruth and Orpah. Naomi bids them to return to their native land. Orpah obeys, reluctantly, but Ruth implores Naomi to allow her to continue the journey with her. Naomi finally consents, and they go forward to-gether.

---

*Only Scene 2 is extant.

# A DRAMATIC SCENE FROM
# THE BIBLICAL STORY OF
# *[THE DEPARTURE OF NAOMI*
# *AND] RUTH*

## SCENE 2.

### Characters—NAOMI, RUTH, and ORPAH

NAOMI:    After many years, I return to Bethlehem, the land of my fathers. There will I end my days, and when the shadows fall, I shall sleep beside my kindred.

RUTH AND ORPAH:    Naomi! Naomi!

NAOMI:    My daughters, why art thou following me? Have I not bidden thee to return to thy native land?

RUTH AND ORPAH:    Leave us not, we pray thee.

NAOMI:    O my beloved ones, have I not said that I have no more sons for thee to marry? Thou art young, and, doubtless, great happiness awaits thee. Canst thou not perceive that the weight of years hath fallen heavily upon me? It is best that I go my way alone.

RUTH:    Say not so, dear Naomi. Surely we will return with thee. We love thee well, is it not true, Orpah?

ORPAH:    'Tis true indeed. And yet I know that Naomi hath spoken wisely, for I feel the call of youth within me. Therefore, O Naomi, I will do as thou hast bidden, and return to my native land. I love thee well, O Naomi, and Ruth, and I shall never forget thee. Farewell.

NAOMI:    Orpah thou has chosen well, and may the Lord bless thee and keep thee, and give thee peace *(Ruth and Naomi raise hands in farewell).*

ORPAH:   The Lord make his face to shine upon thee *(turns away, looks back)*.

NAOMI:   And now, Ruth wilt thou not follow thy sister-in-law?

RUTH:   I care not. I must sojourn with thee.

NAOMI:   My daughter, since thou dost so earnestly desire to share my lot, I can no longer deny thee. Therefore, I say to thee—come, let us journey forward and, tho' many miles stretch their rugged way before us, and e'en tho we become footsore and weary, the Lord God of Israel will not forsake us. He will guide and lead us to the land of our desire. Is this not true, Ruth? His promise never fails. The Lord God of Jacob will renew our strength. We shall run and not be weary, we shall walk and not faint. Thus do we journey in the name of our God *(exit)*.

### THE END

# GLAMOUR VS. BEAUTY

## CAST (THE DREAM-GIRLS' CLUB)

[EDNA]
VIVIAN—*loves glamour*
DOROTHY—*fun-loving*
HELEN—*very dignified, likes to command*
BETTY—*very mischievous*
SYLVIA—*has great desire for physical beauty*
MARION—*very intellectual*
VERA—*likes to pose*
ESTELLE—*Artistic—with pleasing personality*
CELESTE—*very romantic*
HILDA—*calm, thoughtful and modest*
LILLIAN—*haughty and self-conscious*
KEEPER OF THE SHRINE OF BEAUTY
BEAUTY—*who seeks the jewelled crown*
PERSONALITY—*who receives the prize for real beauty*
LITTLE GIFT-BEARER—*who brings the jewelled crown to the Keeper*
MRS. ANGELA AUSTEN—*Sponsor of Youth and Beauty Clubs*

## SCENES

SCENE 1.—*Sylvia's Home*
SCENE 2.—*The Shrine of Beauty (Sylvia's Dream)*
SCENE 3.—*Sylvia's Home*

# SYNOPSIS

The Dream-Girls' Club meets at the home of Sylvia, where they express their own ideas of Beauty, each one hoping to receive the prize for real beauty, which is to be awarded by Mrs. Angela Austen, sponsor of Youth and Beauty Clubs. In Scene 2., Sylvia dreams that she sees the girl who has real beauty, receive the coveted prize—a crown of rare jewels. In Scene 3., Mrs. Angela Austen visits the home of Sylvia, and awards the prize to the most attractive girl.

## SCENE 1. SYLVIA'S HOME

*(Sylvia awaits the coming of the Dream-Girls.)*

SYLVIA: It's almost time for the girls to come *(listen)*[.] I think I hear them now.

*(girls enter noisily)*

GIRLS: Hello, Sylvia, here we are.

SYLVIA: I'm so glad to see you—take off your things.

VIVIAN: We would have been here, before, but Lillian and Vera had to stop and look in all the store windows and admire themselves. They think they are so beautiful.

LILLIAN AND VERA: That isn't true, Vivian.

VIVIAN: Yes, it is, and you both know it. How about it girls?

GIRLS: Of course it's true.

SYLVIA: Now girls, we musn't quarrel. Come, hurry up and sit down. I have some very exciting news. I'm just dying to tell you.

GIRLS: What is it? do tell us.

SYLVIA: Well, Mrs. Angela Austen, sponsor of the Youth and Beauty Clubs, will visit us next Friday night, and the most attractive girl will receive a prize.

GIRLS:    O, really.

SYLVIA:    Yes, it's true, and girls, we shall have to look our best, and be *very* individual.

VIVIAN:    Individual! What does that mean?

HELEN:    Why it means "be yourself" of course.

VIVIAN:    Well, if *that's* what it means, the prize is mine, now, because I'm going to wear my most glamorous outfit that I have, and act the part—like this.

BETTY:    And when Mrs. Angela Austen sees you, she'll say "just another glamour girl."

VIVIAN:    That's all right, Betty, you just wait and see. Now tell us how individual *you* are going to be.

BETTY:    O, I'm going to show Mrs. Austen that I live on the jolly side of life, you know the saying "laugh and the world laughs with you"? I'm sure she will appreciate my captivating smile.

DOROTHY:    You've got something there, Betty. That's the way *I* feel about it, the only thing about it is, that I can't help giggling—everything seems so funny to me.

HELEN:    Well, if you ask me, I am afraid that you and Betty will disgrace us by your silly actions. Now, I'm going to be very dignified, and let Mrs. Austen know that *I* expect to fill a high position in life. *[D]ignity* is *always* attractive.

DOROTHY:    I'm sorry for you, Helen, but you'll have to have more than dignity, to win that prize. Am I right, Betty?

BETTY:    You surely are, Dorothy, but don't worry, our chances for winning are one hundred per cent better than Helen's. *(they laugh)*

VERA:    Dorothy and Betty, I think you are both wrong. Now, I am going to pose gracefully, just like an artist's model. She will admire my attractive figure, don't you think so girls? *(some nod their heads, some look doubtful)*

CELESTE:    Now, *you've* got the wrong idea, Vera. *I'm* the one who will make Mrs. Angela Austen sit up and take notice, you know. I am so romantic, I shall have a languid air. My eyes will be dreamy, just like the movie stars. I know that *I* shall make a tremendous impression. Don't you think so Hilda? You have such *good* judgment.

HILDA:   I wouldn't like to say, Vera, but I shall be glad to see the prize won by any girl who deserves it. I'm sure it won't be my luck to win. I think Celeste has a good chance—she is so artistic, and makes a pleasing appearance.

CELESTE:   I hope Mrs. Austen will think I make a pleasing appearance, but Hilda, the artistic girl is not always the most attractive. Marion, what do you think?

MARION:   I must confess that *I* think the intellectual girl is a good example, and I shall try to use my best [E]nglish for Mrs. Austen, so that she will consider me very well informed and ambitious. Sylvia, we have not heard from you.

SYLVIA:   Girls, I had a strange dream the other night, about real beauty, and it made me doubt my chances for winning the prize. However, I shall try to make myself very attractive in every way. For instance, I know how to use cosmetics, such as the effect of long eye-lashes, the right kind of lipstick, and that alluring rouge, which gives a glowing color to the cheeks. Leave it to me, girls. I'll do my best to win the prize. How about you, Lillian?

LILLIAN:   O, I'm sure that I can easily win. You know I've often been told that *I* have *natural* beauty. I do not have to use make-up. Why Arthur Brown told me just the other day, that I have the [most] beautiful eyes of any girl he has ever seen.

VIVIAN:   Don't you believe it, Lillian.

LILLIAN:   Why not?

VIVIAN:   Because he told me the same thing last night at Estelle's party. *(girls laugh)*

LILLIAN:   O, that doesn't discourage me. I still expect to win the prize. But it's getting late, I think we ought to be going. We promised Professor Fordham, we'd be on time for the rehearsal of our musical program.

GIRLS:   *(putting on their coats)* Yes, let's go. Good-bye Sylvia.

SYLVIA:   Good-bye girls, and be sure to be on time Friday night and look your best.

GIRLS:   We will. *(exit)*

SYLVIA:   *(sitting down by table)* Well, there's no thing certain—we can't all win the prize. *(yawns)* O, I believe I am sleepy. *(drops head on table and falls asleep)*.

**CURTAIN**

# SCENE 2 (SYLVIA'S DREAM)

SCENE—*The Shrine of Beauty*

## Characters

> KEEPER OF THE SHRINE
> LITTLE GIFT-BEARER
> BEAUTY
> PERSONALITY

*(The Keeper of the Shrine of Beauty awaits the coming of the Gift-Seekers. The Little Gift-Bearer brings her the Jewelled Crown to be given to the possessor of real beauty.)*

KEEPER:   Spring is here again. The flowers are blooming and the grass is fresh and green. Soon the Gift-Seekers will be here, anxious to receive the jewelled crown. Ah, here is

Little Gift-Bearer with the precious emblem. *(speaks to her)* I am glad to see you again, little friend.

LITTLE GIFT-BEARER: Thank you, dear Keeper. I have brought the jewelled crown safely to you, from the Royal Palace, and I hope that the one who receives it will be very, very happy, and now, Good-bye, Dear Keeper.

KEEPER: Good-bye, Little Gift-Bearer, I hope we shall meet again next year. *(watches her out of sight then examines the crown)* It is indeed a beautiful crown, and now I shall wait for the coming of the first Seeker. Ah, here she is. *(enter Seeker)* You are welcome. What is your name? and do you seek the jewelled crown?

BEAUTY: I am called Beauty, and I do seek the jewelled crown. I have often been told that my face and form are very beautiful.

KEEPER: And is your face and form all that you have to offer?

BEAUTY: All that I have to offer? Are they not enough? Can you not see that I am very beautiful? why, just look at my silken hair, my smooth skin, and sparking eyes.

KEEPER: You are indeed beautiful, but if time or accident should mar you beauty, what then, will you have to offer your fellow-beings? To win the jewelled crown you must have fadeless beauty. Now, do you understand?

BEAUTY: I—I think I am beginning to see what you mean, and I go my way with a sad heart. Good-bye, O Keeper of the Shrine of Beauty.

KEEPER: Good-bye, dear Seeker, and when you come again to the Shrine of Beauty, I am sure you will have learned the secret of real beauty. *(Beauty disappears)* How strange it is that human beings place such a high value on mere outward beauty, not realizing how quickly it can fade. And now, another Seeker comes to claim the reward. *(enter Personality)*

PERSONALITY:    I am known as Personality, and I am not seeking the jewelled crown, for I have nothing to offer but my desire to learn from you how I can make life beautiful for others. Can you help me?

KEEPER:    I can indeed, because, without knowing it, you possess modesty, kindliness and true culture. The qualities express real beauty, they cannot fade. Therefore, the jewelled crown, rightly belongs to you. *(Personality hesitates)* Nay, do not refuse it, for you deserve this rich reward. *(Place crown on the head of Personality)*

PERSONALITY:    O Keeper of the Shrine of Beauty, I have not words to express my joy. I do not feel worthy of this treasure. But you have taught me a secret of beauty that I shall never forget.

**CURTAIN**

# SCENE 3 (HOME OF SYLVIA)

SYLVIA:    *(meditating)* What a strange dream I had! It has really made me think—O well, I won't tell the girls about it. It might spoil their evening. *(listens)* Here they are now—Hello girls, I'm so glad you're on time. Leave your coats in the hall.

GIRLS:    Hello Sylvia, do we look all right?

SYLVIA:    O yes, except that some of you are made up a little too much.

EDNA:    O, don't worry Sylvia, we only want to look glamorous.

SYLVIA:    All right girls, come, hurry up and sit down. I think Mrs. Austen is coming. *(girls rush to sit down and remain very quiet)*

*(enter Mrs. Austen)*

SYLVIA: How do you do, Mrs. Austen, come right in. May I take your wraps?

MRS. AUSTEN: Thank you. Good-evening, young ladies.

GIRLS: *(rising)* Good-evening, Mrs. Austen.

MRS. AUSTEN: Well, young ladies, I suppose you have been looking forward anxiously to this occasion?

GIRLS: Yes indeed we have.

MRS. AUSTEN: Of course, you know that I am here tonight to give a prize to the most attractive girl. You see I am sponsoring the Youth and Beauty Clubs of our city, in order that we may find out their ideas and opinions of real beauty. Before I award the gifts, I should like to have each young lady demonstrate her idea of beauty by word and action. Suppose we begin with Sylvia.

*(each girl expresses herself)*

SYLVIA: I think that pretty dresses [and] make up look beautiful.

EDNA: And I *know* that beauty must *always* be glamorous.

HELEN: I believe that beauty is *always* dignified.

MARION: My idea of beauty is the intellectual girl, and she must always use *excellent* [E]nglish.

CELESTE: I think the romantic girl is *always* beautiful.

HILDA: I think that a girl can be attractive, if she is neat, courteous and polite.

VERA: A girl can be called beautiful if she is graceful.

ESTELLE: I think the artistic girl is considered beautiful.

BETTY AND DOROTHY: *(arm in arm)* We think a girl is beautiful *(Dorothy giggles)* when she smiles.

LILLIAN: *(walks up and down admiring herself in a mirror)* I think nice features and lovely hair are always beautiful.

MRS. AUSTEN:  *(rising)* Young ladies, I thank you very much for giving me your ideas of beauty, your demonstrations have interested me greatly, and now may I say, that while a beautiful face and form is always pleasing to all of us, and, in these days, we hear a great deal about the glamour girl, we must realize that they are not lasting. Real beauty that is fadeless, consists of modesty, kindliness, charm of manner and true culture. Therefore, it gives me great pleasure to present this prize to Hilda, and I am sure we all agree that she is worthy of it. *(girls applaud)*

HILDA:  O, Mrs. Austen, I hardly know what to say. This is a great surprise to me, and it makes me very, very happy. O, I thank you so much.

*(girls crowd around Hilda saying "isn't it beautiful," etc.)*

EDNA:  I must confess, Hilda, I didn't think you'd get it, but I know, *now*, that after all, glamour doesn't last.

LILLIAN:  And *I* learned my lesson, too.

GIRLS:  And so have we.

SYLVIA:  My dream has really come true.

MRS. AUSTEN:  Young ladies, suppose we give Hilda three cheers: What's the matter with Hilda?

GIRLS:  She's all right.

MRS. AUSTEN:  Who's all right?

GIRLS:  Hilda, Hilda, she's all right. Rah, Rah, Rah.

**CURTAIN**

# A JOLLY THANKSGIVING

SCENE 1. *Home of Marion and her mother*
SCENE 2. *Meeting of the Jolly Dramatic Club*
SCENE 3. *Thanksgiving morning—home of Mildred and her mother*

## CAST

MOTHER
MARION, *the daughter*
[MISS WARDELL,] *Dramatic teacher*
LUCILLE, *pres. of Jolly Dramatic Girls*
HELEN, *secretary*

### Other Members

MARIE     BETTIE     EDITH     ALICE     LINDA

## SCENE 1

*(mother is sewing)*

MOTHER: Marion, why do you look so gloomy tonight?

MARION: Mother, I do not mean to look gloomy, but I was thinking about what you said yesterday about our not having any Thanksgiving dinner. Why do we have to go without one, mother?

207

MOTHER:    Well, Marion, I'll tell you. I have not been able to get sewing enough this year to really pay for a Thanksgiving dinner. I wish we could have it, but we must not worry, Marion. Suppose we look on the bright side, and believe that some door will open for us, shall we?

MARION:    Yes, Mother, I will try to do as you say. I really do not like to worry you.

MOTHER:    That's right, Marion, and now it is time for bed. Good-night, and pleasant dreams.

MARION:    Good-night, Mother.

*(Mother sighs and folds up her work and sits, thinking)*

**CURTAIN**

## SCENE 2

*(Meeting of Jolly Dramatic girls, who are talking with each other)*

LUCILLE:    Come, girls, it is time to open our meeting. Let's sing our club song about smiling.

*(girls sing together)*

LUCILLE:    That sounds good, girls. Now, Helen, please come and take the minutes.

HELEN:    Why I thought we were not going to have regular business, to-day, because we are going to make plans for Thanksgiving.

LUCILLE:    You are right, Helen, but you can take some notes about our plans. Now girls, I've been thinking that at Thanksgiving time, we ought to try to make others happy, don't you think so?

GIRLS:    Yes, we do.

MARIE:    But what shall we do?

LUCILLE: Suppose each one of us ha[s] something to say about it. Edith, what do you think?

EDITH: We might give a party, and make each other happy.

MARIE: Yes, we could, but I think we ought to do something for someone who isn't going to be very happy.

ALICE: You are right, Marie. I only wish we knew someone who isn't going to have anything at all on Thanksgiving day.

LUCILLE: That's a good thought, Alice. What have you to say, Bettie?

BETTIE: O, I don't know of anyone. I only wish I did.

LINDA: O girls, I have it. Marion told me that she couldn't come to the club-meeting to-day, because she has to help her mother. I asked her if she was going to have a Thanksgiving dinner, and she said no, because her mother could not afford it. Couldn't we do something for her?

LUCILLE: O Linda, that's a fine idea. Let's ask Miss Wardell, our dramatic teacher, just the best way to go about it. Here she comes now.

*(Miss Wardell enters)*

MISS WARDELL: How do you do, girls?

GIRLS: Good-afternoon, Miss Wardell.

MISS WARDELL: Well, I suppose you are all making plans for Thanksgiving Day.

LUCILLE: Yes, we are, and we need your help so much. We have just heard that Marion isn't going to have a Thanksgiving dinner. Please tell us how we can help her, and not let her know that the club did it.

MISS WARDELL: Yes, I shall be so glad to help you, and you are right about not letting her know who did it. It will make her happy to realize that others are thinking about her. I would suggest that each one of you give something toward a Thanksgiving dinner, and if there isn't enough money, I will make up the balance. Would you like to do that, girls?

GIRLS: O, yes, Miss Wardell, we'll gladly give something.

*(They give money to Helen, the secretary, who counts it)*

LUCILLE: How much money have we?

MISS WARDELL: That's fine, girls, and I will add two dollars, making it five.

GIRLS: Thank you, Miss Wardell. O, we are so happy.

LUCILLE: Any now, girls, suppose we ask Miss Wardell to buy the dinner the night before Thanksgiving. She knows more about it than we do.

*(Helen gives her the money)*

GIRLS: O, that will be nice.

MISS WARDELL: I'll gladly do so, and you girls can meet me just around the corner from Marion's home. Two girls can take the basket, ring her bell, leave it there, then run back to us before Marion has time to open the door. How will that do? Remember it will be a nine o'clock, Thanksgiving morning.

GIRLS: O, we are so excited.

CURTAIN

# SCENE 3: THANKSGIVING MORNING—HOME OF MARION

*(Miss Wardell and the girls are on the corner)*

MARION: Mother, I guess the girls of our Jolly Dramatic Club will have nice dinners to-day, but I promised not to worry. I am going to try to be real happy to-day.

MOTHER:   That's a good girl, Marion. Our dinner will be very simple, but we are thankful that we have each other, are we not?

MARION:   Yes indeed we are, Mother.

*(Helen and Lucille knock at the door, leave the basket, and run back to the corner.)*

MARION:   O, I think I hear someone knocking. Shall I go to the door, Mother?

MOTHER:   Yes, child. *(Marion opens door—sees the basket—looks all around.)*

MARION:   O Mother, come and help me. Someone has left us a Thanksgiving dinner. I looked up and down the street, but there was no one in sight. I wonder who did it? O, here is a card.

*(Mother helps Marion with basket)*

MOTHER:   What does it say?

MARION:   "To Marion and her mother, sincerely hoping they will have a happy Thanksgiving Day. With every good wish, from your friends." I wonder where it came from? And it's a real dinner, too.

MOTHER:   I am sure I could not guess, but Marion, don't you see that it is always best to look on the bright side, and that we must never lose faith, no matter how dark it looks.

MARION:   Yes, Mother, I do see, and now what a happy, happy day we shall have.

**CURTAIN**

# LOOKING OUT OF THE WINDOW: A DRAMATIC SKETCH

SCENE 1.  *Linda at the living-room window*
SCENE 2.  *The picnic*
SCENE 3.  *Same as scene 1*

## CHARACTERS—

LINDA
LINDA'S MOTHER
PICNICKERS  (BOYS  AND
GIRLS)
DRIVER
MARION
LUCY

This sketch interprets happiness, proper deportment, safety in crossing the streets, and unselfish behavior, such as sharing with each other in games, etc.

## [SCENE 1]

LINDA'S MOTHER:  Linda, Linda, where are you? I have been looking everywhere for you.
LINDA:  Here I am Mother, in the living-room.

MOTHER: *(entering)* Why are you so quiet and what are you doing?

LINDA: I'm just looking out of the window to see if we are going to have a pleasant day, and o, mother, I'm so happy, because the sun is shining.

MOTHER: O, now I see why you are so happy. Linda. It's because this is such a nice day for the picnic. Am I right?

LINDA: Yes, Mother you are right. Isn't it almost time to go?

MOTHER: Yes, Linda. It is time to go. See, I have your lunch all ready. Come let us hurry because we have to meet the boys and girls at the bus station.

LINDA: All right Mother. O, I am so happy. And it is such a lovely day.

## [SCENE 2.] THE PICNIC

PICNICKERS: O, here comes Linda and her mother. We are so glad to see you.

LINDA AND HER MOTHER: And we are so glad to be here. Well, driver, do we stop before we get to the picnic grounds?

DRIVER: Yes, Madam, we stop at Laughing Valley and Running River, so that the children can have some fun along the way.

CHILDREN: O, how nice, driver—now we are off. *(bus starts)*

DRIVER: All off for Running River. *(children scramble off and begin running races and shouting merrily. Mother remains on bus)*

DRIVER: All aboard, Children. *(children hurry back to bus)*.

DRIVER:   All off for Laughing Valley. *(children scramble off and begin laughing, saying "isn't this fun." They swing each other around).*

DRIVER:   All abroad, children, our next stop will be the picnic grounds. *(children rush to bus merrily)*

DRIVER:   Well, here we are at the picnic grounds, all off. Now, Madam I know that you will see that the children get across the street safely.

MOTHER:   Most surely I will. Now children, we must wait here until the green light comes on—there—now we can go safely. We shall walk along orderly and behave correctly. Ah, here is the place where we are to have our picnic. Now you can play some games while I prepare a place for us to each our lunches. *(the children start to play. Marion says, "O, let us play hide-and-seek," Lucy says, "O no, who wants to play that? let's play the-farmer-in-the-dell"—all begin to speak at once, "O, I don't want to play that—")*

MOTHER:   Why children, what is the matter, I thought we came out here to have a nice time. Suppose we play each on[e] of the games, so that all will be satisfied? Wouldn't that be nice?

CHILDREN:   Yes, that is the right thing to do—*(they play each game suggested then, they are called to lunch. They open their boxes and each one begins to eat his own lunch)*

LINDA:   O children, Mother told me that we ought to share with each other, and I am the first one to forget, won't you have some of my sandwiches? *(the children then begin to share, and they enjoy it very much. After lunch they start to play again)*

LINDA'S MOTHER:   Children, suppose we play the game of cleaning up after lunch? Shall we see who can be the first to place our boxes and papers in the park baskets? *(the children shout merrily as they work and soon all is clean where they*

*were eating. They continue their games, until the driver calls*
*"all aboard for home." They wait for Linda's mother to take*
*them across the street)*

MARION:   Let's sing something we all know—*(they sing*
*familiar school songs)*

DRIVER:   Well, here we are just where we started from.
*(children get off, bid each other goody-by.* Linda's mother warns
them about crossing the street)

## [SCENE 3]

MOTHER:   Linda? Did you have a nice time to-day?

LINDA:   O, yes Mother. When I was looking out of the
window this morning, I was so afraid that it was going to
rain, and I did not dream that it would be such a pleasant
sunshiny day.

MOTHER:   Well Linda, that shows that we must try to
look on the bright side, doesn't it?

LINDA:   Yes Mother.

EXIT.

# MAKING CHRIST REAL:
# A VACATION BIBLE SCHOOL PLAY

*by*
*Olivia Ward Bush-Banks*
*(one of the teachers)*

The Play is woven around sacred truths of the reality of Christ. Its Aim is to emphasize the true spirit of worship, and to inspire our Bible School pupils with an earnest desire to make Christ real in their individual lives.

There are Six Scenes and Forty Players.

## CAST OF CHARACTERS

EXPERIENCE—*(recites Prologue and Epilogue)*
STRONGHEART—*(A Seeker of Opportunity)*
SERVICE—*(Unbars the Gate of Opportunity)*
SEED-SOWER—*(Scattering Joy, Courage, Faith and Good-will)*
INSTRUCTORS—*(Recalls "Memories" of Bible School)*
*(Worshippers, Sowers, Good Samaritans,*
*Mischievous Boys, Children of Desire.)*

## *MAKING CHRIST REAL*

## PROLOGUE *(by Experience)*

Dear Friends, I am Experience, and I come to welcome you tonight, as we shall try to reveal to you the Art of Making Christ Real.

You shall listen to the true story of Worship, and witness the Sowers as they sow their seeds of Joy, Courage, Faith and Good-Will. You shall see how every human being can use his talents, and how the Golden Rule can be kept by all who really love our Master. Best of all we shall try to show you [how] loving Service will unbar the Gate of Opportunity, thro' which we can all pass, and ever keep in mind our rich blessings from the King of Kings.


## EPILOGUE *(Experience)*

Again I come to you to thank you for your attention and your interest in our endeavor to please you. And now, our present task is ended. We hope that our efforts have been helpful and inspiring. We as pupils of the Abyssinian Vacation Bible School, desire, more and more to make Christ real in our daily lives, and as the years go on, we trust that the precious lessons we have learned will assist us to become faithful, untiring workers in the Service of the King of Kings.

With grateful hearts we bid you all good-night.


*(Music—opening chorus—"I Think when I read")*

### SCENE 1          Kindergarten Class

## WORSHIP

SCENE *(little girl seated on the platform—children come running in)*

1ST CHILD:   Helen, will you please tell us a story?

GROUP:   O, please do, Helen!

HELEN:    Why, of course I will, children, but what shall it be?

2ND CHILD:    Tell us about Jesus blessing the little children, down by the Sea of Galilee.

HELEN:    All right, children, now come very close and listen. Once upon a time, when Jesus was in Nazareth, a mother, whose name was Hannah, took her four little children, Rachel, Samuel, John and dear little Esther, the baby, to Jesus, down by the Sea of Galilee, that He might bless them. Jesus laid His hands on them, and told them that they were very precious to Him, and He told Hannah, the mother, and Nathan, the father, that it was right for them to bring their children to Him, and that made them all very happy indeed. Did you like the story, dear children?

GROUP:    Yes, Helen, we do, and we thank you so much.

3RD CHILD:    Helen, will Jesus bless us too, if we love Him?

HELEN:    Yes, He will, because we are His precious jewels. Come, let us rise and worship Him.

GROUP:    *(Rising)* Dear Jesus, we thank Thee, that Thou hast said, "Suffer the little children to come unto Me, and forbid them not, for such is the Kingdom of Heaven." Amen.

*(Children go off stage, while School sings Chorus softly, "Like the Stars of the Morning," etc.)*

CURTAIN

## Characters—Eight Children

HELEN, *Story-teller*
1ST, 2ND, 3RD CHILD *and 5 other children in group.*

*(Music—"He Cares for Me")*

## SCENE 2—SOWING GOOD SEED

SCENE—*(The Seed-Sower walks across the Stage and sits down)*

SEED-SOWER:   *(reading)* And Jesus said, "A Sower went forth to sow. Some seed fell by the wayside, and the fowls came and devoured them up. Some fell among the thorns, and the thorns sprang up and choked them. But others fell into good ground and brought forth fruit, some a hundred-fold, some sixty-fold and some thirty-fold."

I wonder what that means? O, I know, one day while I was in the Bible School, our Teacher told us that we too, could sow good seed among our fellow-men. I know what I will do. I'll leave some reminders here for my school-mates, and perhaps I can help them. They'll come along here pretty soon—let me see—I'll just leave Joy, Courage, Faith and Good-Will. Now I must hurry away before they see me. I hope they will find them. *(exit)*

*(group of boys enter)*

1ST BOY:   O! Look, fellows, some one has left Joy here. I think I'll take it along, and it will help me to make some-one else happy. Good-bye fellows *(all say goodbye)*.

2ND BOY:   And here is Courage—just what I need, and I am going to tell other boys about it. I must hurry along. Good-bye. *(exit)*

3RD BOY:   And here is Faith—and I surely need it, because things look so gloomy sometimes, I am going to pass it on to others who need it. I will begin right away. Good-bye, fellows!

4TH BOY:   Well, here I am all alone, but they have left me Good-Will. I can always use this, and it will make a man of me, and teach me to love my fellow-men. I know that the other boys are happy to have Joy, Courage and Faith. I'll go now, and take Good-Will with me, so that I shall be able to sow good seed for others. *(exit)*

CURTAIN

## Characters—Five Boys

SEED-SOWER *(scatters Joy, Courage, Faith and Good-Will)*
1ST BOY—*finds Joy*
2ND BOY—*finds Courage*
3RD BOY—*finds Faith*
4TH BOY—*finds Good-Will*

## SCENE 3          (Quartette)
Recitation

## USING OUR TALENTS

*(SCENE—Mary seated alone, crying. Girls enter laughing and very happy)*

1ST GIRL:   O girls, look! There's Mary. She is crying. Let's go and speak to her.

2ND GIRL:   Why Mary, what is the matter? What are you crying for?

3RD GIRL:   Do tell us Mary, perhaps we can help you.

MARY:   O girls I am so unhappy. I've just been reading where the Master said, "IF we even have one talent, we must use it," but I have no talents at all—not even one, so how can I help anyone?

4TH GIRL:   Why Mary, you can use the talent of kindness, and come with us to see one of our school-mates, who is very sick, and we can cheer her up. Won't you come with us?

5TH GIRL: Yes, do come Mary, and then you will really be doing what Our Master wants you to do. Come, that's a good girl.

MARY: *(rising, smiling)* O girls, of course I'll go with you, and I am so glad that you asked me to. I'll stop and buy some flowers for her and I am sure that it will make her very happy. I never thought of using *kindness* as a talent. O girls you have made me very happy also.

GIRLS: We are all happy, Mary. Come, let us hurry to our school-mate as fast as we can. *(exit)*

CURTAIN

## Characters—Seven Girls

MARY—*(discovers* Kindness *as a Talent)*
1ST GIRL
2ND GIRL
3RD GIRL
4TH GIRL
5TH GIRL

SCENE 4 Solo—National Negro Anthem
Pantomime Class

# THE GOLDEN RULE

SCENE—*(Henry meets a group of boys coming from Bible School. He does not notice a sick man, who has fallen to the ground.)*

1ST BOY: Look fellows! Here come[s] Henry. Wonder where he has been? I say, Henry, why didn't you come to Bible School, today?

HENRY:    Because I didn't want to—that's why. I'll bet you fellows didn't learn one thing today, now did you?

BOYS:    *(all together)* Yes, we did—we always learn something.

HENRY:    O, you do? Ha! Ha! Well, then, tell me what you learned today if you can?

2ND BOY:    We learned how to keep the Golden Rule by helping others.

HENRY:    O, is that so? Well, I don't know anyone who needs my help. Do you?

3RD BOY:    Yes, look over there on the ground, there's a sick man. Come, let's all try to help him up.

HENRY:    O he isn't sick—he's only been drinking, that's all. He doesn't need any help. Ha! Ha! Ha!

4TH BOY:    You don't know that, Henry, and even if he has been drinking, we ought to help him. Come on fellows. Henry, you come too, and help us lift him up.

HENRY:    Well, maybe you're right. *(Boys lift sick man)*

SICK MAN:    O thank you so much boys, I am quite ill. I was trying to get home to my family. I live just around the corner. Will you help me get there? Please?

HENRY:    Yes, indeed we'll help you, and say, fellows, I'm sorry that I spoke so rudely to you, but from now on I shall go to Bible School, because I too, want to keep the Golden Rule. Come on fellows, let's take the sick man home.

CURTAIN

## Characters—Six Boys

HENRY—*(Who stays away from Bible School)*
1ST BOY
2ND BOY

3RD BOY
SICK MAN


*Music—"Jesus Loves Me"*

# SCENE 5    Class

# THE GATE OF OPPORTUNITY

*Theme song—"He is King of Kings"*

SCENE—*(Bad boys bar the Gate of Opportunity before Strongheart comes.)*

1ST BAD BOY: Come on fellows, here comes Strongheart. Let's bar the gate of Opportunity, so that he cannot get thru. Come—quick.

GROUP: All right, we'll help you! *(they bar the gate and run away)*

STRONGHEART: *(whistling—tries the gate)* O, the gate is barred, and now I cannot find the Road of Promise. I want to grow up and become [a] useful man. O, what shall I do? Well I'll wait here awhile and perhaps someone will come and unbar the Gate. *(See[s] children approaching in the distance)* I wonder who these children are? Why, what is the matter, children, who are you, and where do you want to go?

1ST GIRL: *(children crying)* O we are the Children of Desire, and we want to go thro' the Gate of Opportunity and find the way to serve the King of Kings, but the Gate is barred. O, what shall we do?

STRONGHEART: Do not cry, children, perhaps someone will come to help us. O look, here is someone now. *(Enter Service)*

SERVICE:   Why, what is the matter, children (turns to Strongheart) and who are you?

STRONGHEART:   I am Strongheart, and these are the Children of Desire, and we want to go thro' the Gate of Opportunity, and find the way to serve the King of Kings, but someone has barred the Gate. Won't you please help us?

SERVICE:   Yes, dear children, I will gladly help you. I am called "Service," and it is my duty to unbar the Gate of Opportunity for those who wish to serve our King *(unbars the Gate)*. Now, children, do you see that beautiful building in the distance? *(Children reply, "Yes, dear Service.")* Well, follow this road which is called the Road of Promise. Go to the very and where you will find the Bible school, and loving teachers will gladly tell you how best to serve the King of Kings. And now, dear children, Good-bye—God bless you.

CHILDREN:   Good bye, dear Service. We thank you so much.

STRONGHEART:   Come, children, at last we have found the Road of Promise and we shall soon reach the Bible School, and learn how to serve the King of Kings. *(Exit)*

CURTAIN

## Characters—Ten

SERVICE—*Who unbars the Gate of Opportunity*
STRONGHEART—*A Seeker of Opportunity*
CHILDREN OF DESIRE—4      *Leader of Children of Desire*
3 BAD BOYS

*Music—Instrumental—"Blest be the Tie that Binds"*

## SCENE 6   Memories

*Theme song—"Blest be the Tie that Binds"*

SCENE—*(Instructor seated writing is impressed by Theme Song)*

INSTRUCTOR:   *(repeats "Blest be the Tie that Binds.")* Those words are so sweet, and how fitting for such a time as this. Our Bible School closed today, and I have tried to keep a faithful record of our pupils, and the instructions we have given. How pleasant the work has been! I am sure that every teacher has felt like saying at the close of each day:

> One more day's work for Jesus,
> How sweet the work has been.
> And Heaven is nearer, and Christ is dearer,
> Than yesterday to me.
> Lord, if I may, I'll serve another day.

O, I wonder if the pupils have really been helped by our efforts, and if Christ has been made real to them. I earnestly hope so. Ah, here are my girls coming to bid me good-bye *(rises to greet them)*. It's nice of you to come, my dear pupils. I was just thinking about you. Won't you sit down?

GIRLS:   Thank you, dear Teacher.

INSTRUCTOR:   And now, my dear pupils, may I ask if you have enjoyed the Bible School this summer? Suppose each one of you tell me just what it has meant to you. Shall we begin with Helena?

HELENA:   I can hardly find words to express all that the Vacation School has meant to me. I have learned so many valuable lessons, and above all, I have been taught that true worship is not merely lip-service. I realize now, as never before that we really worship when we try to make Christ real in all that we do. I shall never forget the instructions that I received from you and from the other teachers.

INSTRUCTOR:   It makes me very happy, Helena, to hear you express such sincere appreciation, and I am convinced that you now fully realize that true worship lies only in service for the Master.

Margaret, I can see by the happy expression on your face that you, too, have been benefitted by what you have learned during our School session. Won't you tell us about it?

MARGARET:   O, I have so much to be grateful for that I hardly know where to begin. But there is one lesson that I learned, which will remain with me always. It was about "sowing good seed." I have always thought that in order to really help others, we ought to do big things, but now I know that we can find joy in assisting human beings to keep faith and courage, by our own good-will and kind words. I, too, look forward to next summer when our Bible School will open again. I can hardly wait for the time to pass. Will you be with us again next year, dear Teacher?

TEACHER:   Yes, Margaret. I hope to have the privilege of being with you next year, and it makes me more eager, when I hear such encouraging words as Helena and you have spoken. Now Louisa, it is your turn. What have you to tell us?

LOUISE:   I only wish that I had the ability to express what I feel, but I am not capable of doing so. I am reminded, however, of one of the lessons I have learned this summer, concerning "talents." I used to think that I did not have *one* talent, but I have found out that even the least effort we make to help someone can be considered a talent, and by using it we can also keep the Golden Rule. I shall always remember those lessons and try to profit by them.

INSTRUCTOR:   Louise, what you have said inspires me to do my best at all times in training my young pupils, knowing that their whole future depends upon the spiritual foundation which is laid in their youthful years. And now Marion, may we have the parting word from you?

MARION:   I am sure that the girls feel as I do when I say that I find it hard to speak the parting word, for we realize that your instructions and your sympathetic interest will play a valuable part in our lives, and will cause us to render great service to the world in which we live. We are so grateful to you and all of the teachers for opening the Gate of Opportunity, thro' which we have come to the knowledge of "making Christ real" in all that we do. Will you accept our heartfelt thanks?

INSTRUCTOR:   Dear Marion, I am deeply touched by the tribute you have paid me and my co-workers. All that I can say is that I shall always cherish the "memories" of this hour. May God's richest blessings rest always upon each one of you.

God be with you till we meet again? *(Whole School joins in singing)*

CURTAIN

# EPILOGUE—*by Experience*

# FINALE

## Characters—Five

INSTRUCTOR
HELENA—MARGARET—LOUISE—MARION

# THE STAR OF BETHLEHEM *

SCENE 1.—*Shepherds on the plain. . . .*
2.—*The home of Rebecca*
3.—*The manger in Bethlehem*

## CAST

*Shepherds*—DAVID, LEVI, LABAN, REUBEN

*Wise Men*—ARTABAN, CASPAR, MELCHIOR

*Women*—REBECCA, NAOMI, MIRIAM, DORCAS

MARY, *mother of Christ-Child*
JOSEPH

*Herald*—ISHMAEL

## SYNOPSIS

Levi, a shepherd, is waiting for his comrades, who promised to meet him after the sheep were safely gathered in the fold. They arrive—David, Laban and Reuben. David has wonderful things to tell him about a new-born King.

They decide to follow the star, and go to visit the Messiah. Meanwhile Three Wise Men from the East, Artaban, Cas-

* Only scene 1 is extant.

228

par and Melchior, seeking to find the new-born babe, lose their way, and are directed by Ishmael to Bethlehem.

Three women of Bethlehem, Naomi, Mariam and Dorcas, meet at the home of Rebecca where they engage in needlecraft, for the benefit of people who cannot afford to purchase such articles for their homes. Ishmael, whom the Three Wise Men have named Herald o the new-born King, comes hurriedly to the home of Rebecca to acquaint the women with the birth of the Holy Child. They immediately go with Ishmael. In the last scene, Joseph and Mary, and the newborn babe, are visited by the shepherds, the Wise Men, and the Bethlehem women. The scene closes with a hymn of adoration.

*Poem for Intermission*—"Because a Child was Born"
*Music*     "O, Holy Night"
            "Silent Night"
            "O Worship the King"
            "O Come, All Ye Faithful"
            "O, Little Town of Bethlehem"


# THE STAR OF BETHLEHEM

## SCENE 1—SHEPHERDS ON THE PLAIN

LEVI:   I wonder what could have happened to Laban, David and Reuben. I have never known them to tarry so long at their sheep-folds. O, here you are—what has kept thee so long? Has anything happened?

*(David draws apart them, gazing at the sky)*

REUBEN:   Yes, Levi, something did happen—Laban will tell thee about it.

LEVI:   What was it, Laban?

LABAN:    This was it, Levi—David and I had just gotten our sheep in the fold, when we heard Reuben calling to us for help, and we ran to assist him.

LEVI:    Was he in danger, Laban?

LABAN:    No, he was not in danger, but one of his lambs was missing, and he could not find it, so the three of us went in different directions over the plain in search of the poor little creature.

REUBEN:    It was a long search, too, Levi, but after a while, I heard a faint cry and sure enough, there it was caught in a thicket, and could not move. I picked it up tenderly, and called to David and Laban, telling them that at last, I had found my lamb.

LABAN:    O Levi, we were so happy, and after he had fed the lamb, and placed him in the fold with the others, we hurried here, knowing that you would be anxious about us.

LEVI:    Yes, I became very anxious, and I am so glad that you have come. But what is the matter, David—why art thou looking up into the sky? Thou hast not spoken a single word. Art thou troubled about something?

DAVID:    Nay, Levi, I am not troubled. I really feel strangely joyful, for I heard some wonderful news to-day. And I hope it will come true, that is why I was watching the sky.

REUBEN:    Yes, Levi, he did hear some wonderful news. He told Laban and I, and now, he will you thee about it.

*(They gather around David)*

LEVI:    O, tell me, David.

DAVID:    Come, let us sit down on the ground, and I will tell thee—listen—while I was tending my sheep to-day, I saw three strange-looking men, on three camels, riding along the highway. But they seemed worried, as if they [were] not quite sure where they were going. They looked as if they had come from a long distance.

LEVI:   How were they dressed, David?

DAVID:   They were richly dressed in bright-colored Oriental robes, trimmed with gold and silver ornaments. They looked very royal, indeed, and they carried beautiful gifts in their hands. Even their camels had bright-colored blankets on them, and silver bells around their necks. I have never seen a sight like it before. One of the men called to me, saying that he wanted me to help them.

LEVI:   What else did he say to thee, David?

DAVID:   He said that they were wise men from a distant eastern country, and that his name was Artaban, and the other two wise men were Caspar and Melchior. He asked me my name, and I told him it was David, then he introduced me to the others and they bowed so graciously—just as if I had been a prince, instead of a humble shepherd.

LEVI:   Well, hurry up and tell me the wonderful news thou hast spoken of.

DAVID:   Artaban said they were on their way to Bethlehem, to find a new-born babe, and His name would be Jesus and that He would save the people from their sins, and also that He would be called the Savior of the world and the Prince of peace. And Artaban further said that they had been told to cross the plains, and at night, a bright star would appear in the heavens, and lead them to Bethlehem, the place where the Holy Child was born.

REUBEN:   David, tell Levi what they asked thee to do.

DAVID:   He asked me to show them the highway leading to Bethlehem, because evening was coming on, and they did not want to lose their way before the star appeared. So I told them to be sure and take the road to the right, if not they would surely lose their way. Artaban thanked me, then each one of them gave me a precious gem, which I think is worth a very great deal of money—look, are they not beautiful?

*(the shepherds admire them)*

LEVI:   O David, this is wonderful news, and wert thou looking for the star when thou wert gazing up in the sky?

DAVID:   Yes, Levi, I was. O how, I wish that we, too, could go to visit this Holy Child.

LABAN:   We can, we can, the town of Bethlehem is not far from here.

REUBEN:   But what about our sheep?

LEVI:   O, they are safely hidden within the fold—they will sleep the whole night through, and besides we will ask the old shepherd, Jacob, to watch the fold for us, because he has many years upon him, and cannot walk as far as Bethlehem. I am sure that we can go and return before the early morn.

DAVID:   Yes, we can easily do that—O how anxious I am to see the Prince of Peace.

REUBEN:   And so are we. Let us start now.

DAVID:   Nay, Reuben, not now—we shall have to wait for the star to appear.

REUBEN:   O, I forgot that. Of course, we shall have to wait. O, it all seems too wonderful to be true, does it not Laban?

LABAN:   Yes, it is indeed wonderful. But when we go we have no gifts to offer the Holy Child Jesus. The Wise Men had rare and precious gems to give Him.

DAVID:   Do not worry, my comrades. I shall give thee a precious gem that the Wise Men gave me. And I shall present this silver cross to the Prince of Peace *(removes cross from around his neck)*. My mother give it to me when I was just a babe, and I know that she would be glad to have me give it to the Christ-Child.

REUBEN:   O how happy thou hast made us, David. Now we can go as soon as the star appears.

*("Hark! The Herald Angels Sing" is heard)*

LABAN:   Listen, dost thou hear wonderful music?

REUBEN:   Ay, it is indeed glorious.

LEVI:   And now, there are angel voices speaking, listen.

*("Glory to God in the highest—peace on earth, good-will to men")*

DAVID:   *(points to a bright light)*—O comrades, behold a shining light! It is just over us.—It is the star! It is the star!

ALL:   The star! The star! Come, let us go to Bethlehem.

(EXIT)

# A SHANTYTOWN SCANDAL

*Place—Shantytown*                    *Time—any time.*

SCENE 1.    *The Shantytown Women's Current News Club*
SCENE 2.    *The Home of Mrs. Jones*

## CHARACTERS

MRS. ARABELLA JONES—*President of Club*
ALVIRA SMITH—        *Secretary*
BETSEY BROWN—
SALLY DAVIS
JENNIE WILLIAMS—        *a new member*

## SCENE 1. SHANTYTOWN WOMEN'S CURRENT NEWS CLUB

MRS. JONES    *(arranging papers):* It's nearly time for our club meeting *(goes to door)*. O, come right in ladies, I've been wondering if you would be here soon.

WOMEN:    We are so glad to be here.

MRS. JONES:    We shall begin our meeting right away, but we will omit our opening song, because our pianist Miss Becky No-all cannot be with us to-day. Shall we rise and repeat our motto?

ALL TOGETHER: Our *neighbor's* business is *always* our business.

MRS. JONES: Now ladies, I shall ask you to say it again. You know, it is *so* full of meaning. Be sure to emphasize the words "neighbors" and "always."

ALL TOGETHER: Our *NEIGHBOR'S* business is *ALWAYS* our business.

MRS. JONES: Thank you, ladies, that was so much better, and now, Alvira, our secretary will please read the minutes of our last meeting.

MRS. SMITH: Mme. President and ladies, our last meeting was held in our club room February 17, 1939. All of our members brought in news about what was going on here in Shantytown. I do not need to repeat them, but I would like to say that they were not nearly spicy enough. We did not learn much about our neighbors' business, and I sincerely hope that this meeting will be a great deal more exciting and interesting. Collection was twenty-five cents. Respectfully submitted, Alvira Smith.

MRS. JONES: Ladies you have heard the minutes, and, since I hear no objections, I am sure that you accept them. Now, I quite agree with our secretary. Our current news last week were very, very tame. Why, ladies, think of all that is going on around us, inside and outside of our neighbor's homes. We must get busy and bring real spicy news to our club. I hope you have done so to-night. We shall begin with Alvira, our secretary.

ALVIRA: Mme. President, and fellow news-gatherers, I have, at last, found out about Angelina Crabtree's fur coat, she's been boastin about. We thought it cost about one hundred dollars, according to what she said, but it didn't. Because, Mary Ann Johnson was in the bargain store, on Main Street when she bought it. It only cost ten dollars, and it is lined with the cheapest kind of sateen—, and she made us believe that it was lined with real skinners' satin. I examined it, myself when I saw it lying on the bed at Polly Flint's social last night. Now, what do you think of that, ladies?

ALL TOGETHER:    My goodness, how she has deceived us.

MRS. JONES:    Now, Betsey Brown, it's your turn.

MRS. BROWN:    Well, ladies, you know the airs that the Wilson family have been putting on, about their new baby grand piano, and their green brocaded parlor set? Well, the furniture people came and took them away yesterday. I was looking through the blinds and saw them do it, and Tilly Martin told me that Mr. Wilson has lost his job, and now they are on relief. So, ladies it doesn't pay to be so high and mighty, does it?

ALL TOGETHER:    Indeed not.

MRS. JONES:    Ladies, you have indeed brought us the right kind of news, to-day, and I'm sure that Sally Davis has something very exciting to tell us.

MRS. DAVIS:    Yes indeed, I have. I can hardly wait to tell you. Last Tuesday night, when I was coming from prayer-meeting, I saw Sam Green and Lizzie Atkins walking very close together, you know Mrs. Green is visiting her mother [in] Rushville, Mass. And Lizzie Atkins' husband always goes to his lodge meeting on Tuesday evenings. Well, when they got to Lizzie's front door, I hid behind a tree so's I could watch them without them seeing me. They talked a long, long time, and, even tho' it was dark, I was sure that I saw Sam Green kiss Lizzie. Did you ever hear of such goin's on as there is in Shantytown?

ALL TOGETHER:    They ought to be ashamed of themselves.

*(a knock is heard)*

MRS. JONES:     Someone is knocking. Alvira will you please open the door?

*(Alvira goes to door—enter Mrs. Williams)*

MRS. JONES:     O Mrs. Williams, come right in. Ladies, allow me to present Mrs. Jennie Williams who desires to become a member of our club.

ALL TOGETHER:     We are so happy to have you with us, Mrs. Williams.

MRS. WILLIAMS:     I am sorry I'm so late, but I have just come from work, so please excuse me.

MRS. JONES:     That is all right, Mrs. Williams. You are just in time to give us some news items. You know, we are the Shantytown's Women's Current News Club, the only one of its kind in our village, and every member is expected to take part in the meeting, so we will gladly listen to you before we close.

MRS. WILLIAMS:     Mme. President and ladies, I have always been interested in current news. They are so educational, I heard over my radio last night President Roosevelt feels that our country should be prepared, in case of war, even tho' he does believe in peace, and also, that a large sum of money is to be contributed to help the unemployed, and give them more work, isn't that encouraging news, ladies? *(women look disgusted)*

MRS. JONES:     Mrs. Williams, I am sure that you do not quite understand the real object of our club. Our motto is— our neighbor's business is always our business. You see, there are so many things happening here in Shantytown, that we ought to know about so we make every effort to bring all the news we can to our club meetings.

MRS. WILLIAMS:     O excuse me for making such a mistake, Mme. President. Do you mean we must gossip about other people?

MRS. JONES:   O, no indeed, Mrs. Williams, we simply try to know what takes place here in Shantytown. We would not think of gossiping about anyone . . . *(rising)* and now ladies, our meeting is over, and if any of you know anything that even looks like an exciting affair, be sure to come to my house Monday night, and tell me, come ladies—good-night, Mrs. Williams.

*(the women walk scornfully past Mrs. Williams)*

MRS. WILLIAMS:   *(follows slowly)*—Well, well, so that's what they call current news. *(goes out shaking her head)*

**CURTAIN**

## SCENE 2. HOME OF MRS. JONES

MRS. JONES:   Dear me, just look at the holes in these socks? Men always need looking after. Well, I'll darn this one, but it won't do any good.

*(knock is heard—enter Mrs. Smith)*

MRS. SMITH:   Thank you, Mrs. Jones. So glad you are at home. Have you heard the terrible things that have happened down at the Harris's?

MRS. JONES:   Dear me, no. Why they have only been married a year. Do tell me all about it.

MRS. SMITH:   Well, such awful screams are coming out of that house. He's beating her. She screamed for Mrs. Williams to come and help her.

MRS. JONES:   Really? O, it's awful and he looks like butter wouldn't melt in his mouth. I know Mary is sorry that she ever married that Tom Harris.

MRS. SMITH:   You are right, Mrs. Jones, and now I

must go down the street a ways, and see what I can find out *(rising)*.

MRS. JONES: O, do hurry as fast as you can, and come back and tell me all about it. *(she sees Mrs. Brown, and calls for her to come in.)* O, Mrs. Brown, come in quick, I have some terrible news for you.

MRS. BROWN: *(enters—sits down)* What is it? O, tell me all about it.

MRS. JONES: Why, that brute, Tom Harris, has been beating his poor little wife. They say you could hear her from miles around. She had to call for Mrs. Williams to come and help her. Did you ever hear of such a thing?

MRS. BROWN: My, my, this is terrible. *(someone knocks— enter Mrs. Davis)*

MRS. JONES: Come right in, Mrs. Davis. Have you heard the awful news about poor little Mary Harris?

MRS. DAVIS: Yes, I just met Mrs. Smith, and she told me to tell you that she couldn't come back to your house, because she had to hurry home and get dinner for her husband, but she wants you to know that the neighbors saw Mary lying on the floor unconscious from the beating Tom gave her. O, it's awful—here comes Mrs. Williams *(Mrs. Williams knocks)*. Now we'll hear the real truth about it.

MRS. WILLIAMS: Beating her? Why what do you mean? Tom and Mary are just as happy as they can be. I have just left their home. Who told you that dreadful story?

MRS. JONES: Why, Mrs. Smith said that she heard Mary screaming, and that she called you over to come in and help her.

MRS. WILLIAMS: No such a thing, and I think it is a shame the way you women gossip in this town, and that is just why I came over to tell you that I cannot belong to the

Current News Club of Shantytown any longer. You women are too unkind to your neighbors. I'm going now *(rises)* but before I go, I want to ask you a question, Mrs. Jones. When your baby had its first tooth didn't you call the neighbors in, to tell them about it? Well, that's why Mary called me in. Goodbye.

ALL THE WOMEN:    *(looking ashamed)* O, was that it?

CURTAIN

# GREENWICH VILLAGE
# HIGHLIGHTS

Dorothy, you cannot imagine how perfectly lovely it is to have you visiting me tonight, for I've been longing to get the "high up" on Harlem Society and I know that if anyone can tell me, you above all others can, now, let's get real comfy, there now, what [is] the latest? Really, Lucille has a new coat? Persian lamb? I wonder! why, how did she get it? Her husband is only a postal clerk, you know. Aha, I see— but they ar[e] taking desperate chances—goods like that often become liabilities.

Well, what else do you know? What! Maudella has a new car a Sota Fachini? why that's the same make that Peggy Joyce had—it must have cost enormously—How can they afford it? O, how exciting, does her husband know it? Really, well that's a case where ignorance is bliss and absolute folly to be wise. Well, go on, tell me something else that is real spicy. What, you do not know any thing more. [Well] it's my turn, now. I am going to have some highlights on real Society. Of course, you have heard of Will Anthony Madden and his famous Greenwich Village Studio, yes? and you've always longed to meet him? I was sure that you had, I sympathize with you—and it's a great pity that you have to move in the inner circle to be counted among his guests. What sort of affairs does he have? Why, the most exclusive kind, of course, and he always has some ultra-unique features—he is so individual and a real Bohemian. You should have seen his Christmas Party last year—he had a wonderful two-toned Powder Blue Tree that filled a whole corner of his artistic salon, and the color scene of lantern-lights converted the entire Studio into a veritable fairy-land. And he give[s] such beautiful gifts to his guests—and talk about beautiful women, Will Madden always surrounds himself with gorgeous creatures, I do not know where he finds them. They are of every type and exquisite variety.

What does he look like? Now let me see how can I describe him—I assure you, he is easy to look at—Indian brown complexion, a boyish face, and a dangerous, merry twinkle in his eye. He has what one would call a magnetic personality. What did you say [?] O no, he has most skillfully escaped matrimony. Who are his guests on these occasions? Now, let me see—to begin with they are all individualistic in one way or the other, patrons of Art—artists of every known type, temperament thrown in—There is the inimitable Joe Stewart the versatile Joe Stewart, the fascinating Hazel Hughes and a host of others—by the way, do you know that Olivia Ward Bush-Banks? Well I [do] she amuses me— I met her on the street a few days before the *Amsterdam News* Scrapbook Dance, and I said, "What are you going to wear to the Dance, old dear"—she answered with that "air" of hers, "O, my White Chiffon, it's so parisian, you know." Now Dorothy, I do not want to be catty, but as a matter of fact I don't think she has anything else to wear, I saw her with the same "Parisian" gown on two years ago at the Renaissance and the Alhambra. And yet, she is so much of a "free lance" that she had just as soon appear at any function with a Bungalow Apron on—Artistic people are "like that" you know.

O, must you go. I'm sorry, I've enjoyed your being here so much, well the next time I'm visiting friends on "Sugar Hill," I'll call on you and give you the high-light on [t]his New Year's eve. Goodbye, Old Dear, perhaps at some time you will be included within [the] charmed Circle at Will Madden's Famous Greenwich Village Studio, Bye, Bye.

# NEW YEAR MUSINGS

12 o'clock, midnight, 1932! Perhaps I was a bit drowsy, but I surely heard a mysterious voice say "Clinton, have you taken an inventory of last year's failures?" I rubbed my eyes and look around, but I saw no one; So I said lazily, "I suppose you are the Invisible announcer of the New Year, well, Mr. 1933, I have not, because I do not believe in inventories, they are always more or less incorrect and deucedly uninteresting—that is—most of them." "Well,["] said the Invisible One, "what Code of Ethics will you adopt for the New Year?"

"Code of Ethics?" I replied. "Just what do you mean by that? new resolutions?" "Exactly," said the Unseen One[.] "O, if that's what you mean I'll tell you a few things that I plan to do in the interest of Higher Education.

"First, I resolve to attend all of the Friday Night Classes. To leave the school each night with the same hat and coat that I wore there, and it might not be a bad idea for me to go to school bare-headed, and thereby lessen the duties of the Service Squad.

"To chew tobacco, instead of smoking, since it is less dangerous to the school-building.

"I'll try to appear interested in the high-falutin words of the *Odyssey*, because Mr. Cowan's efforts ought to be appreciated more than they are.

"As for Mrs. Shelly, our Spanish teacher, I realize that I'll have to give her better lessons this year, so that I can see a look of approval on her face, rather than the critical expression, which makes one feel thoroughly ashamed of himself, and sends cold shivers down his spine.

"I may insert a new plank in my political platform which will at least give me a balance where the hyphenated American is concerned, for, after all, true patriotism makes us differentiate between our social preferences and our civic responsibilities. Perhaps this proposed change of attitude on my part may serve as a foundation for commendable classroom ethics. Is there anything wrong with this Code, Mr. 1933[?"]

The Invisible One said, "O the Code is all right, Clinton,—only hope you'll live up to it, but there is one thing more—are you going to spread gloom this year, or are you going to wear the golden smile? And what about the 'New Deal'?"

"Don't worry, Mr. 1933, even tho' I don't give the 'golden smile,' I'll try to put just a little brightness into that much-talked of 'New Deal,' by recognizing that no revised form of government or redistributed wealth can give us a 'new deal' in life, unless we ourselves are ready for it, and the only way to get it is to go out and dig for it—then we'll surely be on our way again towards winning back our common sense. I know what hard work, plain living and less superficiality will make us 'regular folks' and we can defy Old Man Depression and say to him,—

> [']Your time is up, old sober-sides,
> So run away and hide your face,
> You can't come back again, because
> Prosperity sits in your place. [' "]

# THANKSGIVING REVERIE

## THE COLONISTS

A home in the wilderness. Within that crude structure, are pilgrim pioneers gathered around an open fire-place. Glowing embers light up the faces of those sturdy adventurers, who in search of religious freedom braved a perilous ocean voyage, even to the rock-bound coast of New England.

It is Thanksgiving Eve, and undisturbed by the distant roar of [angry?] waters, lashing a bleak and sandy shore, or the surging winds through pathless forests, they sit in reverie—recounting the dangers passed, deeply conscious of stupendous tasks awaiting them. They pledge themselves, unsparingly to a new and hazardous life—felling mighty oaks, making trails through the trackless forests, tilling the soil, and rearing safe dwellings for their wives and offspring.

Doubtless, they envision the sure foundation of a great Republic, its citizens will conform to law and order, its economic life shall be strengthened by inventive and creative efforts, and its social and spiritual attainments become ideal standards for human living.

For all this, and for the new opportunity now unfolding, they give heartfelt thanks, while the fire-light dims, and dying embers lose their ruddy glow.

## 1932

Thanksgiving Eve. The tumult of a great metropolis. Flashing lights, majestic structures rearing their lofty heights on the Island of Manhattan. Teeming throngs of pleasure-seekers, treading the magic "Great White Way."

Alone, in a Fifth Avenue mansion, a successful financier, sits by an electric gas-log, reflecting upon the high civilization of modern life. A veritable speed-age—with air-plane and dirigible as the master-accomplishments. The panorama of "Big Business" reveals a great Automobile Industry, the Romance of Wall Street—the startling innovations of Wireless Telegraphy, Radio achievements, tel-e-vision, and other incredible actualities.

He muses thoughtfully—"Where is the utopian Republic envisioned by those pilgrim pioneers?" Surely the reign of gangsters, racketeers, the murk and mire of political exploitation, and the rumblings of bloody warfare, have no place within the virgin realm of colonial idealism."

Could he give thanks? yes, for marvellous material advancements. But, the great Republic, unsullied by greed and selfishness, as yet, does not exist. The dream of the pioneer remains unfulfilled.

The slight pressure of a button, and the artificial fire-flame disappears. He retires amid luxurious surroundings—restless and perplexed.

# BLACK COMMUNISM

SCENE—midnight—Columbus Circle, N.Y. Bread-line, grim, graphic, challenging.

Wyatt Hendricks, an attractive, dark brown Harlemite, surveyed with sympathetic interest, the endless line of job-less, hunger-stricken men. Yes, he quite understood the revolutionary re-action of some of his fellow-beings. It was the inevitable—obviously the one way out—blood must be shed!

Suddenly his reflections were rudely interrupted by the menacing shouts of on-coming, avenging Communists, who surged threateningly around the van of food, supplied by the city's emotional philanthropy. With ever-increasing wrath, they overturned cartons of sandwiches, hurling forth invectives, "Down the rich!" "Down with the mockery of charity doling out its damnable hypocrisy, while wealth flaunts by with flashing diamonds, wasting its millions in lavish luxuries. Curses on them!"

Wyatt Hendricks recalled vividly, a Communist parade through the heart of Harlem—the flaring banners "Lynching in America must go!" "Labor knows no color line!" "Help us to avenge the injustice to our dead, black comrade." How his blood tingled! here was justice, first-hand. Why should his people continue to endure the fiendish practices of south-ern injustices? He conjured up the horrible scenes of his helpless, tortured race down in Georgia and Mississippi, where the very atmosphere fairly reeked with the stench of roasting flesh. Were his people cowards of the basest sort? Did they really have red blood in their veins? He remembered that he had started to join the dauntless marchers in Harlem—hesitated—What had restrained him? Was it that he preferred a bloodless victory? Was the economic life of his people strong enough to demand, through such drastic measures, their God-given right to "fair play"? Should he besmirch the stainless records of dark Americans, who had so heroically maintained their standard of loyalty to law and order during two hundred years of the mockery of American freedom?

At this point something fell heavily at his feet—a large carton of sandwiches. He seized it—struggled through the writhing mob—on around the corner of a quiet thoroughfare, and began rapidly passing sandwiches to the famished ones of the un-employed. They surrounded him—"Say, young fellow, you're doing a good work" "God bless you" "You've got red blood in your veins" "You're all right, Buddie." The supply was quickly exhausted. Wyatt, realizing that his role, as a dispenser of charity was not ended, made his way quickly with difficulty thro' the increasing number of followers, and finally succeeded in boarding an elevated train, en route to Harlem. His humanity had proven as strong as the "New Democracy" that "is to be," yes, even stronger than his bitter hatred of his Country's infidelity.

# WHAT ABOUT OUR LOYAL COLORED AMERICANS?

Our country has accorded the Japanese people every right that belongs to American citizens. They have filled our colleges, they have received every possible encouragement in the development and pursuit of their artistic inheritances, contributions to the realm of Art.

They have been given social distinction among the best white families of our country. In the matter of employment they have been given precedent over Colored Americans in positions of trust, even in the homes of fine white Americans, where loyalty is a sacred essential. Colored American employees hithertofor used in our Railroad Service throughout the country have been replaced by Japanese.

And now, how have they returned these unlimited privileges? By the dastardly commitment of treachery, deceit and disloyalty.

Has our country forgotten the record of Colored Americans to whom they entrusted their homes and beloved families in the dark days of the Civil War? Has the Colored American ever plotted against our government[?] Has he not endured patiently, undeserved discrimination and injustice heaped upon him, even at the present time? In all the nation's conflicts, has he not gone forth, even as he is now, demonstrating the true spirit of democratic service?

Is not this flagrant exposition of Japanese perfidy, sufficient to prove that we need Colored American loyalty as never before in the history of our beloved country[?] Americans All, awake! awake!

# AUNT VINEY'S SKETCHES

Aunt Viney, a Negro Woman, is a welcome and frequent visitor at Miss Ollie's gift-shop, which she calls drift-shop, because, as she puts it, the wood that drifts down the river dont help to make the nice warm fire but it is that which drifts in on the shore, that keeps the winter cold out of the house. Likewise, the people that help to earn Miss Ollie her bread and butter—not those that drift on past.

Aunt Viney has a keen sense of humor, and a quaint philosophy of her own, consequently, she is amusingly interesting whenever she visits Miss Ollie's shop.

* 1. Aunt Viney Names Miss Ollie's Gift-shop, and Talks on Art.
   2. Aunt Viney Starts for Atlantic City, and Ends Up at Coney Island.
   3. Aunt Viney Tells of Her Visit to [the] Beauty Shop, and Also Announces Her Engagement to Mose Hardup.
* 4. Aunt Viney Talks on Harlem Society, and the Depression.
* 5. Aunt Viney Talks on Negro Spirituals.
* 6. Aunt Viney Declares That in These Days, Even the Church is a Racket.
* [7. Aunt Viney Tells of an Interesting Sunday in Harlem.]

* The starred episodes of *Aunt Viney's Sketches* appeared in a special issue of the *Langston Hughes Review* 6, no. 2 (1987): 1–10.

# AUNT VINEY NAMES MISS OLLIE'S GIFT-SHOP, AND TALKS ON ART

*(Miss Ollie is singing as she arranges novelties in gift-shop. Enter Aunt Viney complaining of the heat.)*

AUNT VINEY:   Mawnin' Miss Ollie.

MISS OLLIE:   I'm feeling fine, Aunt Viney, and I hope you are, too.

AUNT VINEY:   O honey I would be feelin' good, but I'se *so* warm.

MISS OLLIE:   Here's a fan, Aunt Viney, and won't you have some powder?

AUNT VINEY:   I thanks you fo' the fan, Miss Ollie, but what does I want wid de powder?

MISS OLLIE:   Why, to take the shine off you face.

AUNT VINEY:   Tek de shine offen my face? Why honey chile, what is you talkin' 'bout? I reckon you don't read your Bible much, does you?

MISS OLLIE:   Why of course I do, but what has that to do with using face powder?

AUNT VINEY:   It's got a plenty to do wid it. Ef I 'members right, 'bout ennything at all 'en de Good Book, it says over dere in the fust part, 'bout dat man, Moses, who got mad 'en broke de stone where he had de Ten Commandments all to pieces, 'en de Book also says dat he had been talkin' wid God Almight, up dere on de mountain, 'en when he cum down, his face shine so bright, dat de people cud'dnt look at him. He didn't use no face powder—is I enny better den Moses?

MISS OLLIE:   Oh Aunt Viney, you are really too funny for anything. That's why I am always so glad to see you. I love to have you come here—you're just like a ray of sunshine.

AUNT VINEY:   'En I likes to come too, Miss Ollie, now dat I knows you better. When I fust seed you, I thought you wuz one of dose high-powered incorrectibles.

MISS OLLIE:   Incorrectibles? Why Aunt Viney, you mean intellectuals, don't you?

AUNT VINEY:   No I doesn't. I means incorrectibles—dem peoples what knows eberyting, 'en dey ain't nobody libin' dat kin tell 'em ennything—dat's what I means. But you ain't like dat, at all, Miss Ollie—you's jes plain folks, 'en dat's why I like to come to the drift-shop.

MISS OLLIE:   Drift-shop, Aunt Viney? You mean gift-shop.

AUNT VINEY:   No, no honey, I means jes what I says— drift-shop. Ain't you neber libed down by de sea-sho,' 'en seed de driftwood drift by?

MISS OLLIE:   Why of course, Aunt Viney. I spent all my last summer in my uncle's cottage, in Groton, Connecticut. He lives right on the shore, and I used to go out every morning, and help him pick up the driftwood.

AUNT VINEY:   Well, den, honey, you knows dat de wood what went on floatin' down de ribber, didn't do you 'en your uncle no good. But de wood dat drifted in on de sho' made de bright warm fire, when de nights wuz col', didn't it?

MISS OLLIE:   Of course, you are right about that, Aunt Viney.

AUNT VINEY:   Yes, 'en I'se right when I calls you place de drift-shop, coz, it ain't de people dat drifts on pas' here, dat you wants—it's dem what drifts in 'en spends dey money wid you. Say honey, I sutinly likes de looks ob dis place, tho' I offen wonder why dese drift-shops has so many curious tings in em: ladies wid no arms, 'en marble folks wid wings on em, 'en 'ol three-legged tables dat dey calls an-ti-ques. Well, I guess dey's what people wants, or dey wud'dent be here.

But honey, ez I look aroun' I don't see no Monin' Lizzy. Is you got one?

MISS OLLIE:   Monin' Lizzy? What do you mean, Aunt Viney?

AUNT VINEY:   See here chile, does you mean to tell me dat you ain't neber seed de picter ob Monin' Lizzy? Dat gal where looks likes she's tinkin' up debilment, 'en nobody's eber been able to tell wedder she's smilin' or fixin' to git all de money som' po' man's been wurkin' hard fo' all his days? I neber did trus' de smile in dat gal's face. 'En you see her picter in all de sto's, 'en rich folks pays all kind of money, jes' to say dat dey's got a Monin' Lizzy. I th'ot sho' you'de hab one here—I'se s'prized, did I is.

MISS OLLIE:   O Aunt Viney, now I know what you are talking about. You mean Mona Lisa. Yes, I ought to have a picture of her. You are right.

AUNT VINEY:   Dat's right, honey, dat's who it is. I th'ot you'd know who she am. Well, I must go now, chile. I'se had a good rest. Now don't forget—it am de people what comes in dis drift-shop, 'en not de people dat walks on pas', dat he'p you git yo' bread 'n butter. Bye bye, honey. I'se comin' again, real soon.

MISS OLLIE:   Aunt Viney, take care of yourself, and come whenever you want to.


# AUNT VINEY STARTS FOR ATLANTIC CITY, AND ENDS UP AT CONEY ISLAND

AUNT VINEY:   Mawnin' Miss Ollie.

MISS OLLIE:   Good morning, Aunt Viney—why, what's

the matter, You have a real blue Monday expression on your face.

AUNT VINEY:    Is I? Well, dis aint no red-letter day with me, 'en yestiddy wuzzent no glorious week-end.

MISS OLLIE:    Come now, Aunt Viney, cheer up, and tell me all about it. Did you go to Atlantic City?

AUNT VINEY:    Well, I started dere, but I ended up at dat Coney Island.

MISS OLLIE:    Coney Island? Why, how did that happen?

AUNT VINEY:    You see, 'twas like dis. Dat crazy frien' of mine, Sallie Noall, tole me dat dey wuz a 'scursion to 'lantic City, 'en it only cost $2.00 to git dere 'en back. So I gits up at 6, yestiddy mawnin' puts on dat red 'en yaller spote dress ob mine 'en my white shoes, dat wuz a size too small for me, takes my green silk umbrella, 'en gits on de subway at de corner of a Hunerd 25th St. 'en Lennox Ave. 'En goes to de Penn Station, wher I meets Sally Noall 'en we gits on de train.

MISS OLLIE:    Well, you got a good start Aunt Viney, didn't you?

AUNT VINEY:    Yes, Miss Ollie, I got a good start all right, but de train we wuz on, stiddy stoppin' at de Penn Station, went right on pas' 'en I says to Sallie, "we's pas' de station," but Sally, who cant see so well, 'en pretends she kin, says "No we is'nt, 'en I knows what I'se doin' so lebe it to me." So I lebes it to her; but when de conductor, calls out "Las stop" in de subway, we gits out 'en goes up-stairs, 'en dere we wuz, way down to de Battery, where all de big steamboats goes out.

MISS OLLIE:    Down at the Battery? I know you must have been somewhat disappointed, Aunt Viney.

AUNT VINEY:    Dis'pinted? I wuz mad thoo' 'en thoo', but, Sally, she says "O, I'se only made a little mistake." So back we gits on de train goin' up town, 'en gits of[f] at de Penn

Station, but it wuz 8:40 en de train wuz s'posed to lebe at 8:45, so we had to run to git to de ticket office, en my po feet wuz all swell up in dem tight shoes. Sally axed de ticket-man fo two tickets to 'lantic City, he says, "Woman, dat 'scursion went las' Sunday mawnin', 'en day aint goin' to be no more 'scursions 'twell next August."

Miss Ollie:   What did you do then, Aunt Viney?

Aunt Viney:   I didn't know what to do or say, Miss Ollie, but when de ticket man said, "Ef you wants to go to Atlantic City in de nex' two minits, I kin sell you a one-way ticket fo' three dollars," I speaks up, 'en says, "No suh, I dont want to go, coz, I'se only got $2.50 'en I'se dun spent 15 cents ob dat tryin' to fine de way back from de Battery to de Penn Station. Come on, Sally, let's git de fust train dat comes, 'en go home, coz' my feet is 'bout to kill me." So we gits on de train, 'en keeps on ridin' 'twell de conductor calls out "All off fo' Coney Island, dis train dont go no furder."

Miss Ollie:   What an experience! Aunt Viney, now I know why you look so gloomy to-day. Did you have a good time at Coney Island?

Aunt Viney:   Good time, Miss Ollie? I neber wants to see dat place agin. I neber seed such a crowd in all my life. Well bime-by we gits to de merry-go-roun' 'en Sall[ie] says, "Come, lets hab a ride," but I says, "You kin ride 'ef you wants to, but I aint goin to spend 5 cents to git my haid all dizzy, goin' roun' 'en roun' on dem fool hosses." So I goes 'en sits down. But ef you believe me, dat Sallie Noall spent 25 cents fo she got offen dat hoss.

Miss Ollie:   Well, Sall[ie] must have had a wonderful time, Aunt Viney, according to what you tell me.

Aunt Viney:   She sutin'ly did, coz' she kep' spendin' money. Why, she axed me to buy a hot dog, at only ten cents a piece, after dat, she bought a ice-cream cone, a lolipop, 'en two glasses ob sody water. Den she wanted me to go on dat roller coaster, where goes so fas' dat you cant eben see where you'se goin' or what you'se lookin' at. I says to her, "No, coz' I'se dun spent so much now, dat I'se fraid I cant git back to de city, so good-buy, I'se goin home."

MISS OLLIE:    Was Sall[ie] ready to go home, Aunt Viney?

AUNT VINEY:    No, she wuzzent ready to go, coz' she got awful mad wid me. But she come along jes' the same. When we got outen de subway at Lennox Ave. my feet wuz swelled up so bad, dat I had to take off my shoes 'en stockings 'en walk home. Ob cose it wuz dark, 'en so wuz my feet, so nobody noticed me. I wuz glad to git home, Miss Ollie, did I wuz.

MISS OLLIE:    Poor Aunt Viney, I know how you must have felt. But what became of your friend, Sall[ie]?

AUNT VINEY:    Dat gal? She lef' me at 125th 'en Lennox Ave. 'en the las' I seed ob her, she wuz buyin' two pig feet, 'en half a watermelon to take home. I dont know what kind of a stomach, dat gal has, but one thing I does know, she'll neber member seein' me any mo' at dat Coney Island, I dont care how many times she starts to go on dat 'lantic City 'scursion. Well, good-bye, Miss Ollie, I mus' go now. I'll stop by tomorrer mawnin' 'en say, Howdy.

MISS OLLIE:    All right, Aunt Viney, I'll be looking for you, and I hope you won't have the blues any more.


## AUNT VINEY TELLS OF HER VISIT TO THE BEAUTY SHOP, AND ALSO ANNOUNCES HER ENGAGEMENT TO MOSE HARDUP

AUNT VINEY:    Mawnin' Miss Ollie, I hopes you'se feelin' well dis mawnin'.

MISS OLLIE:  Good Morning, Aunt Viney, I'm feeling very well. How are you?

AUNT VINEY:  O, I ain't no power-house dis mawnin', but I'se had some funny 'speriences.

MISS OLLIE:  Oh, do tell me about them, Aunt Viney.

AUNT VINEY:  Well, fust place, I went to one ob dem beauty shops dis mawnin' to git my hair fixed up, 'en I says to de gal, I wants some hair to wear on Sunday, but doan't bu'n off de little I'se got here, and de gal she says, "Don't you want me to touch it up wid a little dye? It makes you look younger." En I sez, "No, I doesn't, coz I'se got a frien' now who tried to look younger, en she dyed her hair, en had some of dat henna stuff on it, 'en now she don't look like nuthin' coz she didn't hab money to keep it up. And de hair has turned all green en brown, en de gray is showin' at de roots, looks to me like she'll neber git it to look natchral agin. No suh!" I'd rudder look as ol' ez Methusalah, den to hab all dem colors on my haid. But Miss Ollie, dat gal sho' did mek my haid look gran', en dat how come I to git a proposal.

MISS OLLIE:  Proposal! Aunt Viney, what do you mean?

AUNT VINEY:  I means jes what I sez,—I'se engaged to be mai'ed.

MISS OLLIE:  Engaged? Well, who's the lucky man?

AUNT VINEY:  Why, its Mose Hardup, 'en he said I look so good wid my haid all slicked down, 'en den he says, "Viney, I wants you fo myself. Will you mai'ey me?"

MISS OLLIE:  And what did you say, Aunt Viney?

AUNT VINEY:  Well, Miss Ollie, I pretends like I'se bashful, en den I sez, softlike, "No."

MISS OLLIE:  You said no, Aunt Viney? Why, you are not engaged if that's your answer.

AUNT VINEY:  Yes, I *is* engaged, coz when a woman sez no she means yes—ain't dat so? At lease dat's what Mose sez, en he's gwine to gib me a ring, fo I changes my mind.

MISS OLLIE:    Change your mind? Why Aunt Viney, you wouldn't be as fickle as that, would you?

AUNT VINEY:    I dunno. You see, its all de style now. All dem Hollywood gals, changes dey minds like dey change deir cloes, but don't you worry Miss Ollie, we isn't goin to git hitched up right away, coz we's both on relief now, en you knows dat dis relief and dis lub bizness don't go toged-der somehow, so Mose is gwine to git hissef a job, although the Lord knows when dat will be, diz ever'body is gittin' dem pink slips now, Well, de good Lord still lives, en he kin open doors dat no man kin shut.

MISS OLLIE:    I see that you have great faith, Aunt Vi-ney, and I do hope that when you do get married, you will both be very happy.

AUNT VINEY:    Thanks, Miss Ollie. I hopes so, too. Well, I must be gittin' along now, 'en stop by the doctor's coz I'se got a pain, en I'se afraid dat I'se gittin an appendix. I'll see you tomorror. Good-by.

MISS OLLIE:    Goodbye, Aunt Viney. Be sure to come tomorrow. I hope you won't get that "appendix."


## AUNT VINEY TALKS ON HARLEM SOCIETY, AND THE DEPRESSION

AUNT VINEY:    Mawnin' Miss Ollie.

MISS OLLIE:    Good morning, Aunt Viney, you look happy. What has happened?

AUNT VINEY:    O Miss Ollie, I heered the funniest ting this mawnin'. I nigh 'bout split my sides laffin.

MISS OLLIE:    Do tell me about it, Aunt Viney.

AUNT VINEY:    Well, I walked behind two cullud men on my way down here, and dey wuz talkin' 'bout Harlem society. 'En one of 'em sez, "I wuz invited up to a frien' of mine yestiddy, on Sugar Hill, where de rent is $90.00 a month, 'en when dinnertime cum, he sez, won't you hab some lemonade en crackers? Well, man, I wuz hungry, but I wanted to be polite, so I sez, yes indeed, 'en when he opened dat frigid ice-box to get de one lemon dat he had, dere wuzzen't eben an inch of hot dawg in dere; 'en I knows well dat he cud'dnt find eben one grain in his coffee can if he scrapped twell doomesday. Well, after he had de lemonade wid a pinch ob sugar, 'en two Uneeda biscuits, I sez goodbye 'en went to see anoder frien' of mine where libs downtown on de corner ob 5th Avenue 'en Madison; 'en say, he gib me a gang ob beef-stew, hot co'n bread, coffee 'en apple pie, 'en pays $30.00 a month. Now, dats what I calls real libin', en its good enuff fer me. Tell me 'bout yo Harlem society." Well, Miss Ollie, he sutinly tol' de truff. But wuzzen't dat funny?

MISS OLLIE: Yes, Aunt Viney, I can really see the funny side of that. It's enough to make anyone laugh. Now, what else have you to tell me?

AUNT VINEY: Miss Ollie, I'se been tinking 'bout the Depression, 'en 'bout how some ob my people is boun' to keep up wid de Joneses.

MISS OLLIE: What do you mean, Aunt Viney?

AUNT VINEY: I means dis—I wuz libin' in Chicago, when de Depression fust started, 'en some of de banks failed. I heered some of my folks say, "Does you know dat I loss ebery penny I had in de worl' when de bank went broke?" Now Miss Ollie, I found out dat a heap ob dem, has jes $1.00 in dere. Ain't dat sumpin'?

But de times has changed since den, coz, now, dese same people has been on de A.B.C.'s, en de WPA,s, 'en dey's ridin' aroun' in streamline kyars, 'en de wimmin is wearin' dose gon wid de win dresses. 'En look like a million dollars, but dey better look out; 'coz de time is right now, when dey's gittin' dese pink slips, 'en dey won't hab eny mo' chance to stan' in de pay-roll line, 'en walk away with dim blue checks. Dey sho' will hab to go back on relief. Now speakin' 'bout de relief, I can't talk against it, coz' I'se on it myself, 'en its bin a great hep' to me, tho' I'de rather hab work coz' it makes enybody feel so much mo' independent. But I'se feared dat dis relief hez been a mighty bad ting for some ob dese lazy cullud men. Stidy tryin' to git wuk, dey sits down home 'en waits for de food 'en de rent check. Bit I knows plenty cullud women dat goes out 'en tries to get days work, so dat dere chillen kin hab shoes 'en warm clothes to wear. I'se really feared dat dis relief hab made some of dese men mo' wuthless dan dey wuz fo' de Depression.

But Miss Ollie, dere's lots ob good cullud 'en white folks, too, who am tryin' to mek de bes' ob tings in dese tryin' times. Sometimes I tink dat de cullud folks don't feel it ez bad as de white folks, coz, my people knowed all about de Depression, long before it hit dis country. We's always been depressed, but we don't git weary or discouraged—we jes keeps on singing 'en hopin. Well, its time for me to go. O say, de doctor said dat I wuzzen't gittin' no appendix—'twas nothin' but gas. I sho' was glad, Miss Ollie.

Miss Ollie:    I'm glad for you, Aunt Viney. Goodbye— I'll look for you tomorrow.


## AUNT VINEY TALKS ON NEGRO SPIRITUALS


Aunt Viney:    Here I is agin, Miss Ollie. I sutinly like to come to yo drift-shop.

Miss Ollie:    And I am always so happy to see you, Aunt

Viney. You have so many interesting things to talk about. Where were you last night, Aunt Viney?

AUNT VINEY:   O, I wuz at the Triump Baptist Church las' night to hear de songs ob our people[.]   . . .

MISS OLLIE:   You mean the American Negro Spirituals.

AUNT VINEY:   Yes, I guess dat's de high-falutin' way ob s'pressin it, but I like to call 'em de jubilee songs, coz most ob 'em is happy songs, eben do dis race hab had some sad times 'en is still habin' em, we's happy folks jes de same. Dat meks me tink—dis concert wuz in de Triump Baptist Chu'ch en if you notice, our folks always names our chu'ches after somethin' that sounds happy. Why, a frien' of mine said dat las' Sunday she went out to de country, 'en went to fo' different chu'ches, 'en de names wuz Mawnin' Star Baptist Chu'ch, Mt. Zion, Mt. Air-at, 'en Mt. Eagle. Well, dose names show dat we'se always lookin' upward.

Now about de jubilee songs—I'se feared some ob our folks is gittin' off from de way our mothers 'en fathers used to sing 'em. In de fust place, day don't need no piano, coz it's jus' de natchral voice dat meks de white folks pat dey noses to keep dey tears back. But when dey sang "Steal Away to Jesus" 'las night, I know well enuff dat dem high-tricklin' notes neber belonged in dere. It sounded too much like oprey, you calls it. Den, dey had a gospel singer, 'en de way she jazzed up dem songs! I felt jes' like gittin' up 'en doing' a two-step, deed I did. Coz, dat jazz musick meks you feel peppy, bit it sho' don't do sinner eny good. I know dey'd neber git me up to eny morner's bench, coz I cud'dnt keep my feet still long enuff. I jes' didn't like de way dey carried on, so I went home fo' it was ober. But we's libin' in a day when dey meks a dance tune out ob eberyting. Why, I'se eben heered dem jazzing "De Holy City," en dat pretty song 'bout a tree dat looks at God all day, and dat piece of music called leib-her-lone—why, it's awful.

MISS OLLIE:    You mean "Liebestraume," don't you, Aunt Viney?

AUNT VINEY:    Yes, dat's it. I ain't bery good at gittin' de names, but I knows and lubs de music when I hears it. Now, to git back to de jubilee songs. Miss Ollie, does you eber listen at de white folks tryin' to sing dem over de radio? 'En does you tink that they really sings 'em like cullud folks does?

MISS OLLIE:    Yes, Aunt Viney, I often listen to them, and I must confess that they do not sound quite like your people's way of singing them. What do you think about it, Aunt Viney?

AUNT VINEY:    Well, I agrees wid you, Miss Ollie, but I'se noticed dat dey's tryin' mighty hard to put de cullud touch to dese songs. Why, dey's all over Harlem, in de cullud chu'ches, listenin' to de singin' 'en does you know that some of 'em is gittin' pretty nigh doin' jes' like our folks. You know, Miss Ollie, I'se mighty proud of our jubilee songs, coz dey is de only American songs dat white and black folks hab in dis country. 'En jes' to tink, dey wuz made up by our mothers 'en fathers way back in slavery times when dey wuzzent 'lowed to learn readin' en writin'. So I tells my people day eny race what can gib music to a big country like dis, dey surely will git on top some day, don't you tink so, Miss Ollie.

MISS OLLIE:    Yes, Aunt Viney, they surely will. Why, already they are making great progress.

AUNT VINEY:    Dat's true, 'en dey is doin' somethin' besides singin'. Dey's writin' books, on cullud history, 'en poetry, 'en we's eben got science men such as dat George Washington Carver, down dere in Alabama. Why he's mekin' all kinds of oil out of peanuts 'en sweet 'tatoes, 'en de las' ting he's done is find de way to git somethin' dat will he'p po little chillen 'en keep 'em from bein' so sick, wid dat awful p'ralises. What does you call it, Miss Ollie?

MISS OLLIE: Infantile paralysis, that's what you're trying to say, Aunt Viney?

AUNT VINEY: Dat's right, Miss Ollie—I 'clare you knows eberyting. Well, I'se proud dat I belongs to dis race, 'en I ain't neber goin' to try to git away from it. Ob course, eny-body dat has the kind of tan dat I'se got on my face, kin never be enything else but jes' plain cullud . . . Well, Miss Ollie, I really mus' stop talkin' 'en go buy some bacon en greens, fo da sto's close. Goodbye, honey.

MISS OLLIE: Goodbye, Aunt Viney—be sure to come tomorrow.

## AUNT VINEY DECLARES THAT IN THESE DAYS, EVEN THE CHURCH IS A RACKET

AUNT VINEY: Mawnin', Miss Ollie.

MISS OLLIE: Good morning, Aunt Viney. I am glad to see you. What have you been thinking about, since I saw you last Monday?

AUNT VINEY: Well, Miss Ollie, I'se been tinking dat in dese days, eben de chu'ch is gittin' to be an awful racket. Why, I know a minister who had a baptizin' las' summer, 'en he had a foto-graph man standin' on de bank takin pic-ter's ob every candidate that went in de water, so he cud sell 'em to de members and friends ob de chu'ch 'en mek money to he'p pay on de new house he wuz buildin'. What does you tink of dat, Miss Ollie?

MISS OLLIE: Well, it seems to me that he was more interested in his own selfish motives than he was in such a sacred thing as baptism.

AUNT VINEY: You sutinly is right, Miss Ollie. He axed

me to buy one, but I tole him dat I wuzzent goin' to he'p him, nor any udder pasture to sell out de Mastah's business, 'en it don't say enything 'bout mekin' money otten a baptism in de Holy Bible, so de pasture kin git hissef a new bung'low. 'En dere's annuder reason why I says de chu'ch is gittin' to be a racket, Miss Ollie.

MISS OLLIE:    I'd really like to know just what your other reason is, Aunt Viney—do tell me.

AUNT VINEY:    It's dis—I 'members a watchmeetin' I went to las' year, 'en it wuz crowded to de do's, 'en de preacher had people jes' screamin' 'en shoutin' 'bout de lub ob God, 'en how we ought to be libin' 'samples fo sinnahs, 'en de deacons sho' wuz kep busy, pickin' up de wimmin, 'en cal'en dem to de ante-room, coz dey fainted from shoutin' or pretended dat dey did. 'En it looked to me dat de deacons wuz busiest wid de good-lookin' sisters, 'en de sisters seemed to git bery happy when dey foun' demselves in de arms ob de decons.

MISS OLLIE:    Why Aunt Viney, I have never heard anything like that before. The meeting must have been very exciting.

AUNT VINEY:    'Deed it wuz, Miss Ollie, 'en it went on dat way unteel jes' befo' midnight, when de people from de Harlem sportin' wurl' begin to crowd in, coz dey belibes dat dey ought to spen' de las' minits ob de ol' year in de chu'ch. Now de preacher knowed dat spotes always has plenty money, so he says in a trimblin' voice—"De ole year is 'mos gone, so at dis point in de meetin' we must show de Mastah dat we really knows how to serve Him, 'en I wants everybody to come up to dis table 'en put down a big collection—I knows dat dere is plenty money hyar to-night."

MISS OLLIE:    And did the people really give him a good collection?

AUNT VINEY: DID they? Well suh, dey jes' crowded up dar, 'en when dey got thru' dere wuz mo' dan $300.000 on de table. Den I says to myself, "Now de preacher will gib out de invitation fo' sinnahs to cum to de monah's bench, 'en fine Christ precious to dere souls," coz dere wuz many dere dat needed to be sabed. But Miss Ollie, all dat cullud preacher said wuz, 'It am one minit to midnight, 'en I wants dat de New Year fine's us on our feet, shoutin' 'en praisin' Gwad fo' dis big collection dat will he'p de pasture to hab plenty to eat 'en drink, to ca'ey on de wuk ob de Gospel. I wishes everybody a Happy New Year!"

MISS OLLIE: Why Aunt Viney, that does look like a racket, as you call it, because that was a splendid opportunity for the pastor to help those people from the underworld.

AUNT VINEY: 'Deed it wuz, Miss Ollie. Well, sich shoutin' 'en actin' up, I neber did see, 'en Miss Ollie, dere wuzzent one word said 'bout tryin' to sabe de souls ob dem spotes. It jes' made me hyart-sick, 'en dats why I says dat some ob de chu'ches is nuthin' but a big racket.

Cose, dey's a heap ob good people, 'en some real hones' preachers, but dere's a heap ob racketeerin' goin on[.] . . . Well Miss Ollie, I guess dat I'se talked enuff 'bout rackets, but I'se glad to git dis off my mind, 'en you is so understan-din', Miss Ollie.

MISS OLLIE: I try to be, Aunt Viney, and I do realize that we do not always find true religion in the church, but we must try to see the good side of everything in this life.

AUNT VINEY: Dat's so, Miss Ollie—You'se right—you always hep's me so much. Well, I guess I'll be gittin 'lon towards home. Goodbye, honey, I hopes to see you agin dis week.

MISS OLLIE: Goodbye, Aunt Viney, don't stay away too long.

# AUNT VINEY TELLS OF AN INTERESTING SUNDAY IN HARLEM

AUNT VINEY:    Mawnin', Miss Ollie, how is you on dis blue Monday mawnin?

MISS OLLIE:    I'm feeling fine, Aunt Viney, and it isn't blue Monday with me at all. How is it with you?

AUNT VINEY:    O, I'se fine too, specially after yestiddy, coz I sutinly had one interestin' Sunday. I dunno when I'se laffed so much from de time I heered de sermon at one ob de Baptis' chu'ches in de mawnin', up to de parade I seed in de ebenin, leastways it was almos' night.

MISS OLLIE:    Do tell me all about it, Aunt Viney. What was so funny about the sermon you heard?

AUNT VINEY:    Well, Miss Ollie, 'twas like dis[.] . . . By de way, did you ever see dat play, called "pogey"?

MISS OLLIE:    You mean "Porgy" don't you, Aunt Viney?

AUNT VINEY:    Yes, dat's de name. I'se always gittin' mixed up when it comes to names. You say you has seen it?

MISS OLLIE:    Yes, I saw it as a play and also as an opera, but what connection has it with the sermon?

AUNT VINEY:    Lawdy Miss Ollie, it had a whole heap to do wid it, coz de preacher-man took his tex' from it. *(Laughs heartily.)* Lawdy!

MISS OLLIE:    Took his text from "Porgy"? What could it have been?

AUNT VINEY:    Well, b'leve it or not his tex' was, "You'se got plenty of nothin'." It was a scream, Miss Ollie, from de beginnin' to de endin'. Fust he tole about de man in de Bible dat had a heap of money and a lot of barns filled wid all kinds of good tings to eat and it look as if t'would las' him 'twell de Judgement Day, so he sez to his family 'en friends, "Let you souls be at ease, 'jes eat, drink 'en be merry, coz

I'se got plenty ob eberyting," but de good Lawd heered him talkin' so big, 'en what do you tink He tole dat onery man?

MISS OLLIE: Aunt Viney, I cannot even imagine what the Master could have said.

AUNT VINEY: Well, Miss Ollie, de Master sez, "You'se all wrong, Mr. Man, coz all you'se got is plenty of nothin', and you can't eben take dat wid you, an another ting, you'se got to die tonight anyway." Well suh dat preacher-man went on from dere and tole de people dat folks haz got de wrong idea 'bout what dey's got coz what they calls *something*—is just nothin' at all. Dey get a lot of furniture 'en big cars what dey cain't pay fo, an din dey buys up a lot of something to eat, such as big slabs of meat 'en taters, 'en black-eyed peas, 'en dey tells all dere friens "Ise living on de top o' de worl', come in and hep yo self." But when de Lawd sent fo them, dey couldn't take eny ob dat stuff wid 'em. O Miss Ollie, de way he tole dat, made me nearly split my sides a'laffin.

MISS OLLIE: What else did he say?

AUNT VINEY: Well, he ended up by sayin' dat some people tink dat becoz, dey's givin' a lot of money to de chu'ch, 'en bin a big member ob' de decon bo'd dey can go up to Hiben, 'en tell 'postle Paul dat dey too has "fought a good fite," but Paul will look ober de record books 'en say, "Who is you? I doan even see yo name. Go on down where you belongs, coz you ain't done nothin' wirth'while, you ain't got nothin', 'en nothin' belongs to you up here—'en you cain't expec' black-eyed peas dat you had down dere to lan' you safe in Glory."

MISS OLLIE *(laughing heartily):* Aunt Viney, I can easily understand why that sermon made you laugh. Now, tell me about the parade you saw.

AUNT VINEY: Miss Ollie, you don know cullud folks

like I does, but I'm tellin' you dey sholy lubs to parade. Yestiddy dey had what de call the "Black Jews" parade up 'en down 7th Avenue, 'en dey wore de African robes of all colors 'en carried de African Flag, 'en it wuz a sight to behold. 'En dey eben had a great big Flag, 'en dey eben had a great big picter of Haly Selassy on dere.

It was hot az blazen, dey marched jis de same, 'en de band played out in dat burnin' sun untwell ebery las' one ob dem marched into de big ball room, corner 183rd Street 'en 7th Avenue. 'En what does you tink, Miss Ollie, dere wuz a lot of white folks marchin' wid em, and dey carried big signs dat meant dey wuzn't goin' to stan' fo eny mo serimination against black folks. You know, Miss Ollie, somehow dese days whereeber you sees cullud folks tryin' to help derselves you'll see white folks wid 'em.

Oh, I forgot to say dat dere was one of de Black Jews ridin up 'en down down on a firy horse 'en war dressed like Haley Selassy, and he looked like he owned de whole ob New York City. You know, Miss Ollie, it doan take *dis* much to mek some folk act big when dey really ain't nothin' at all.

So you see, I had a bery interesting Sunday, and when I went to bed las' night, I sez to myself, "Did I eber expec' to lib to see de day, when dere would be enuff real Black Jews to make a big parade like what I seed to-day," 'en when I got to tinking 'bout de sermon en de black-eyed peas, I got to laffin' so I jes' cud'dnt say my prayers. Well, good by, honey, see you to-morrer mawnin.

Miss Ollie:    Good-bye Aunt Viney, and I hope you will have many more interesting Sundays to tell me about. You bring me a great deal of cheer and always a new light on life's meaning.

# UNPUBLISHED WORKS: MEMOIRS
## *c. 1935–1944*

❧ ❧ ❧

*Although repetitive in language and structure,* The Lure of the Distances *vividly portrays Bush-Banks's life and times. She cultivated a variety of friends who, like her, possessed cosmopolitan, artistic, and spiritual natures. Over the years these associations fortified her with the emotional sustenance she needed to persist creatively. In this respect, Chapter 4 is especially relevant as evidence of the Negro Renaissance in Chicago. Also intriguing is Bush-Banks's consistent substitution of the word* comradeship *for* friendship. *This probably signifies a socialist influence and also connotes her deeply rooted need for these relationships.*

*Likewise, her daughter and granddaughter (Marie and Helen Horton, respectively), occupy a revered place in the memoirs. Bush-Banks lived with them periodically during the last two decades of her life while her second husband served as a Pullman porter. The two younger women en-*

couraged her in her work. (Incidentally, Marie and Helen were Seventh Day Adventists [Helen is still active in the denomination], and they witnessed Bush-Banks's conversion to the faith shortly before her death.) It is not known if Bush-Banks made a serious attempt to publish the memoirs.

One sad domestic note was Bush-Banks's estrangement from her other daughter, Rosa Olivia (Rosamund) Bush Lockhart. Personality clashes and Bush-Bank's dislike of Rosa's husband contributed to ill feelings. Rosa Olivia died in 1929, and there is no mention of her or her descendants in the memoirs.

The reader will note that Chapter 1, "Distances," is missing. It is not known if Bush-Banks ever actually wrote the chapter or if it has been lost, although as suggested earlier, two autobiographical notations found in the Bush-Banks Papers at Tulane University may have been intended for part of the chapter.

## DEDICATION:

To my Aunt
Maria Draper

Who loved me unceasingly
  Labored untiringly
  Sacrificed willingly her own
Life's interests, this book is most
affectionately dedicated.

# THE LURE OF THE DISTANCES

*by*
*Olivia Ward Bush-Banks*

## APOSTROPHE

Not in vain have I waited thro' near and distant years to make known the rich fruitage of Life's experiences; golden memories, and dreams fulfilled, in my quest for the universal touch with fellow-beings.

## FOR[E]W[O]RD

Distances fascinate me. Far horizons, glowing heights of mountain majesty, picturesque levels of serene valleys, broad highways, winding paths, and the gleaming expanse of boundless oceans have always created within me a desire for adventure, discovery and exploration.

Even more alluring have been the seeming distances between human varieties with their distinctive types, shades of coloring and engaging personalities, always revealing and emphasizing the nearness of relationships held in common.

Most happily have I been surrounded by this refreshing atmosphere, without obviously inviting it, during all the understanding years of my life. Such a rare privilege may be accounted for thro' the vagaries of birth. With my background of American Indian and Negro parentage I have keenly felt the urge of commingled ancestral calls within me, thro' which, doubtless, I have been enabled to recognize the similarity of emotions, desires and behavior in other humans.

Therefore, paying tribute to those who have so heartily welcomed me within the alluring realm of genuine comradeship, I venture to portray, thro' these intimated narratives, and poetic expression the nearness of apparent human distances.

OLIVIA WARD BUSH-BANKS

## CHAPTERS

1. —Distances
2. —Lights 'o' the Trail
3. —The Gleam and the Glow
4. —Steady Beacons
5. —Heights
6. —Fragrant Pathways
7. —Serene Valleys
8. —Lamps at Even

The above chapters are expressed in narrative form including the following nationalities with whom I have enjoyed close contacts of fine fellowship. They are, namely,—English, Italian, American Indian, Jew[ish], Irish, White and Colored Americans, Persian, German, Mexican and Russian. 11 Nationalities—30 characters.

## Chapter 2
## LIGHTS 'O' THE TRAIL

### Marion Lychenheim Block

Life often leads us over unexpected trails within the realm of Nature. Sometimes, by refreshing streams of sparkling waters or thro' flower' scented fields, again thro' cool green forests, where murmuring trees, seem to bid us rest awhile in peace and contentment (err?) we take our way through Earth's crowded places. While these experiences are delightful they cannot be compared to the overwhelming sense of gratitude one feels for the rare privilege of following the trails that lead to the fireside of true com[r]ades.

Marion Lychenheim was a veritable Light 'o' the trail, and her cheery little homestead in the Rogers Park section of Chicago, reflected the glowing light on Marion's face as she welcomed varied coterie of comrades who followed many trails to her home-place.

I cannot adequately interpret the joy and satisfaction of being counted among Marion's guests, or the precious memory of those delightful evenings, when musical art and literature thrilled us to the very depths of our souls. Sometimes we listened to the magnificent baritone voice of John Greene, or to stirring orchestral strains under Marion's direction, and were lifted to higher planes of living by poetical interpretations of inspired authors.

### Florence Willis

Florence Willis was, by inheritance, unmistakably Anglo-Saxon, but I preferred to think of her as a rare combination of many physical and spiritual inheritances. In her contacts, she manifested an overwhelming passion for human varieties, and because she also knew so well the fine art of living, moved with delightful ease among them.

She was a veritable light 'o' the trail, a venturesome seeker of interesting types and for some indefinable reason, seemed to enjoy selecting me as a comrade to share her unique explorations. Again and again I found myself seated by her side among audiences of exotic Orientals or inhabitants from the Isles of the sea, and from the distances of Earth's far places. As a devotee of Art, she revelled in their colorful aspects, their native genius, counting them all as invaluable contributors to the fascinating realms of human living.

Somehow, I recognized this fine individual as one who had come from some higher plane of existence bringing with her an atmosphere of unchanging love for all mortals regardless of humble origin or racial handicaps. I have found great joy in following the trails of life that she has made both possible and passable by sending forth the enduring light of her genuine love of humankind.

## Chapter 3
## THE GLEAM AND THE GLOW

### Southern Hospitality

I have had delightful experiences in various sections of the southland, where I came in touch with a number of warmhearted friends. In the Educational center of Atlanta, Ga, as a guest of Atlanta University Morehouse and Spelman Colleges[,] I shall ever retain the memory of the hearty welcome

I received from the late Professor John Hope, Pres. of Morehouse College, whom I knew so well when he was a Student at Brown University, Providence, R.I. He was always a source of inspiration to me when ever I had the privilege of speaking with him. When I visited Fiske University, and Meharry Medical Colleges in Nashville, Tennessee, I was accorded every courtesy, through the kindness of Dr. Lester, Dean of Physicians at Meharry. The same gracious treatment was repeated by Dr. Dudley[,] President of A. and T. College, Greensboro, North Carolina. And at Hampton Virginia, Mayor Washington, the distinguished Commandant, and Dr. Finneger, Chaplain of that institution and his friendly wife spared no pains in making me feel very much at home on southern soil.

My visit to Richmond, VA, was memorable indeed because of the hospitable attitude of that magnificent distinguished woman Maggie Walker, founder of a notable business enterprise offering employment to many capable women of all ages. Mme Walker was deeply interested in my dramatic programs of Indian life, and she followed up this interest by introducing me to an audience of more than 2,000 people, urging them to become patrons of my Play—*The Trail of the Montauk*. It was my privilege also while in Richmond to be the guest of Mrs. Ruffin, Ex. Sec. of the Y.W.C.A. and through her kind favor I had the extreme pleasure of witnessing "The White Christmas," an annual celebration at Hartshorn Memorial College, one of the finest institutions of learning in Virginia.

From Richmond, I visited Norfolk where I was graciously received by Prof. Jaycox, Principal of Booker Washington High School, and given the privilege of presenting my Indian Play—*The Trail of the Montauk* with a cast of 25 beautiful girls, who were obviously pleased to cooperate with me.

Our play was a real success, financially and otherwise. It assisted in replenishing the School Library, much to Prof. Jaycox and [?] satisfaction.

(While all of these contacts I have mentioned afforded me valuable educational information for which I was deeply grateful, no experience however cherished could transcend my sojourn in the heart of Catawba Mountains, Virginia[.])

The Catawba Sanatorium, located about twenty miles from Roanoke Va, was indeed picturesquely surrounded and I shall long remember the welcome invitation of its Supt. who instructed a young student to escort me all through the various departments of the Sanatorium and the out-of-door surroundings. I even had the privilege of conversing with the patients and I found the whole atmosphere pervaded by the spirit of true friendliness. Added to this experience, after following a trail thro a veritable lane of leaves where the scent of pine-trees lingered, I was received so heartily in the little one-room cabins of those kindly mountaineers, some of whom had never been in touch with the world outside of the "hills of home." I recall vividly an evening spent at the farm-house owned by Mr. and Mrs. Jones[,] two of the oldest residents on Catawba. It was storming furiously on the outside, but, as I sat with my host and hostess around a blazing fire-place, and listened to the reminiscences of the man of the house, while pattering rain-drops made music on the roof, I knew that I was the recipient of a rare privilege one could never enjoy in the crowded ways of city life. After listening to the sweet strains of evening, I slept peacefully within the white-washed walls of their little guest-chamber until the morning sun gleamed through thro' the weather-beaten logs. As an expression of the inspiration I received, I pay tribute in the following lines

*Catawba*

O Memory, again I wander
Thru the Realm of Unforgotten Days,
I tread upon the downy softness
of a lane of leaves
Where the scent of pine trees [lingers]

pleasant [?]. My heart burns within me, as I recall the contacts with friends in the south-land, who demonstrated so genuinely the spirit of true comradeship toward the Stranger within these days [?].

# Forrista Bowman (Danbury, Conn.)

One of the most striking illustrations of rare comradeship that I have ever known was Forrista Bowman, who enjoyed the delightful period of thirty or more years.

Surrounded by the picturesque background of Danbury, Conn. where she was an outstanding presence in the life [of] the community she kept alive her native gift of a song-bird of unusual quality.

Forrista, in her physical aspect, was as artistic as the name she bore. Distinctly Indian in type, and yet, evidencing the warmth and colorful characteristics of darker Americans, she possessed a subtle magnetism that was positively compelling.

As a guest in her uniquely attractive home, one breathed in the atmosphere of congeniality and sincerity of a hearty welcome. She was a versatile exponent of the fine art of living possessing an appreciable amount of physical flexibility that was delightful to observe. For example, one afternoon, while entertaining a lively group of happy, glamorous girls I noted that Forrista joined heartily and gracefully in their rythmic demonstration of modern social dancing, her lithe figure swaying in utter abandon, her eyes sparking with the joy of it all. Just as her spirit seemed to effervesce and overflow her physical being, so the sweetness of her voice seemed to transcend its tone in all the emotional variation of songs, which she rendered divinely.

Added to all this was her native capacity for dispensing human kindness. As I reposed restfully in her charming guest room I could readily discern her love for the beautiful which she so happily combined with artistic comforts, that seemed to reverberate with the unmistakable declaration "You are a welcome guest. ["]

Surely the nearness of her genuine concern for the happiness of others shall ever abide with me, lighting up the ways of life whenever darkness threatens to throw its gloomy shadows across my pathway. The gleam and the glow of Forrista's charming personality will always remain in my memory, a constant reminder of one who leads a comrade over pleasant trails.

## Mildred Lunde (To be completed)

One summer evening in the long ago, while passing thro' a small New England village, I noted the cheerful glow of lights, streaming from the windows of attractive little homes, and I also caught gleaming lights here and there, on the hillside, giving evidence of happy family life far removed from the stress and strain of city habitation. Somehow I found real pleasure in comparing the gleam and glow with friends, who, unconsciously lend brightness to us along Life's winding ways. Mildred Lunde had a way of sending forth gleams of goodwill and friendly interest, in her contact with other humans.

Whenever I visited Riverside Hospital, situated in North

Brothers' Island, N.Y. Miss Lunde, who for ten years served as Director of Nursing extended me a hearty welcome to sit beneath the shade-trees, where I was refreshed by cool breezes, and to enjoy rare sunsets shedding their crimson glow over the rippling waters[.]

Miss Lunde possessed a rare sense of humor, that was delightfully apparent in spite of her close contact with human suffering and the endless responsibilities of her official position. She was obviously of Norwegian birth, with a background of fine ancestral inheritances, which undoubtedly accounted for her inestimable traits of character.

Her gracious favors, have more than once, set my heart a-glow, and I am sure she never quite realized how deeply I have prized her friendly acts of genuine human kindness.

She was an ardent enthusiast in promoting social contacts in the interest of [unintelligible phrase].

One glorious autumn day when I was one of Mildred Lunde's guests on the occasion of dedicating the new hospital at Riverside where many noted officials gathered to assist in laying the cornerstone of that magnificent structure [unfinished.]

## On the Dunes of Indiana with Margaret Cross

Margaret Cross was unmistakably Irish, with auburn hair and deep-blue eyes. I shall never forget my sojourn in her fascinating little Bungalow, near the sand[-d]unes of Indiana.

It was the Autumn-time and we wandered daily around the red and golden glory of tree-covered woods on our way to the silent dunes.

I had always thought of sand-dunes only as low mounds of drifted sand, but I was overwhelmed by the sight of picturesque, undulating hills, and as we climbed them our feet sank deep in the shifting sands. When we reached the summit, before us lay a veritable desert of gleaming white sand, far-reaching and sublime in aspect.

Every moment of those vacation days spent with Margaret Cross in her cozy bungalow at the foot of those fascinating dunes, remains clear and outstanding in my memory.

Margaret was so obviously committed to the joy of giving me happy vacation moments, that she sought every opportunity for this fulfillment. As an illustration of her fine desire, we fared forth one glorious moonlight night to witness the rare spectacle of an expansive green, grassy level, over which a magic mantle of blue-white mist seemed to settle with indefinable loveliness. With the light of the moon above us, and this veritable sea of mist at our feet, we found ourselves completely under the subtle spell of a holy calmness—transcending all earthly surroundings. The scene was indescribable. As we turned our footsteps homeward, Margaret's face was radiant with the consciousness of my grateful, unuttered acceptance of this scene of exquisite beauty, which even as I write, sees to re-appear in all of its splendrous reality.

I must also make mention of an incident which portrayed Margaret's loyalty to democratic ideals. On one occasion she gave a dinner party for the late James Weldon Johnson in the ultra down-town section of Chicago, Ill. and as one of her guests I can never forget her procedure in arranging the couples as she purposely led us along Michigan Ave. Margaret's companion was one of the Guests of Honor of the National Association for the advancement of Colored People. I was asked to walk with a representative from the Land of the Orient, while an attractive English lady walked proudly by the side of a Brown American, of journalistic fame. Arriving at the unique Colonial Inn, we were the center of attraction, much to the delight of Margaret who expressed herself in this manner[:] "Michigan Ave. has had an unmistakable evidence of real Democracy today. ["]

Whenever I think of Margaret Cross, she stands forth in my memory as a shining light in true Americanism. When I reflect upon her loving attitude toward me, I know, again the joyousness of wandering with her through the realm of Unforgotten Days, over the dune-hills of Indiana[.]

## Michael Rosenberg

Russian Michael Rosenberg, who preferred to be called Mike, was a fair-haired, blue-eyed young Jew with fine intellectual aspirations, and pronounced inhibitions pertaining to human justice. His scathing denunciations of a so-called democracy were very interesting to me. One of his favorite recollections was that of his trip through the south-land, during which he decided to pass for a Col red American that he might learn the actual fact of discrimination against his fellow-beings who were forced to ride in separate coaches. The word picture he painted of that experience was both pathetic and amusing.

When I asked him how he concealed his blond hair, he replied[, "]I pulled my cap tightly over my ears, entered the coach, and told the conductor who questioned me again and again, that I was of Negro and white parentage, and when he insisted that I looked white, and I must leave the coach, I reminded him of a fixed law in some southern states, that an individual known to have one drop of Negro blood could not under any circumstances be allowed to ride in a coach with white passengers. The conductor reluctantly went his way, and I was free to continue my journey, unmolested by him. ["]

I shall refrain from relating Mike's indignant portrayal of that experience, but I am still wondering how he dared to venture on such a mission, in spite of his unmistakable white skin, blue eyes and fair hair. Mike was indeed an interesting comrade, having acquired a fund of literary knowledge, and he was thoroughly coversant with International history, thus giving him a splendid background for his scientific deductions[.]

His long cherished dream of returning to Russia to enter the conflict for right-and justice was eventually fulfilled. If he accomplished the desired end, I do not know. I only know that he was a courageous defender of fair play in the interest of all humanity, and as such, I counted him a valuable friend and comrade within the Realm of goodly fellowship.

## Will Anthony Madden

Greenwich Village! the very mention of which recalls delightful experiences as a guest in the Studios of Will Anthony Madden where one was fairly submerged in the atmosphere of rare camaraderie and artistic identity.

Will Madden was a real Villager, having first seen the light of day as an infant in this uniquely romantic section of New York City.

The fact of his birth, augmented by his intriguing personality and delightful abandon in thought and action gave him an enviable background for surrounding himself with fellow humans of many physical varieties who revelled in the privilege of contact with him, welcoming every occasion to follow the trail to his open doorway.

Chapter 4
# STEADY BEACONS

## Lincoln Center Comrades

When Jenkins Lloyd Jones, that fine loyal humanitarian founded Abraham Lincoln Center in Chicago over 25 years ago as an open door for all who believed in brotherhood, undoubtedly he did not dream of its far-reaching influence, or the lights it would shed on the paths and by-paths of those whose privilege it was to pass within its sacred walls.

There it stands on the corner of Oakwood Boulevard and Langley Ave, a majestic monument to educational advancement and kindred fellowship, and I found my way eagerly to its rich privileges on every possible occasion. What a flood of memories come over me as I think of the weekly Friday morning Forum, when I listened to men and women of national and international repute from every part of the Globe. How these messages burned their way deep into my very soul! And, always the noon-hours proved a happy climax when we enjoyed the pleasant experience of dining together. There I discovered real comrades, whose friendship remained true thro' the years. Among them, Mrs. Helen Rosenfels, our delightful hostess, and program director extended her fine hospitality to me through many acts of kindness, sometimes an invitation to classical recitals, making it possible for me to come in close contact with outstanding [unintelligible], again bidding me welcome to her home in Oak Park, where we engaged in pleasant discussions of interests which we held in common. She, always manifesting a loving and encouraging concern in my aspirations, and a sympathetic attitude toward human problems confronting me.

Lillian Olf—Lillian Olf, a fair-haired, New Englander, and a prolific Writer, welcomed me always within the realm of her warm-hearted interest. The doors of her home were always open to me, and through her I was the happy recipient of many helpful contacts. It was she who introduced me to John Haynes Holmes[,] that fearless defender of human rights. Mrs. Olf, knowing that I planned to become a citizen of New York City, wrote Mr. Holmes to that effect, and he immediately gave me a cordial invitation to visit his Community Church, and as a result I enjoyed a membership of seven years under the fine leadership of Mr. Holmes until I was called upon to assume responsibilities in another section of the city.

Lincoln Center afforded me the opportunity of fulfilling my literary desires in the presentation of Dramatic programs, and creative demonstrations among the neighborhood's young people.

Best of all, the Center inspired me with its genuine spirit of comradeship towards all individuals and groups, regardless of nationality or condition.

Because of the rich benefits I received from such uplifting association I with countless others pay high tribute to its illustrious founder who so obviously believed in the nearness of seemingly human distances.

## John Haynes Holmes

If one were asked to give the proper setting to the life and aims of John Haynes Holmes, one would immediately characterize him as a friend to man. Such was my impression upon meeting him 14 years ago at Abraham Lincoln Center, Chicago, Ill. and hearing him give a stirring talk touching the human side of Life's affairs. Later it was my privilege to contact him for eight years as a member of his Community Church, New York City.

During those years I was thoroughly convinced that Mr. Holmes knew no racial distances between human beings.

I listened every Sunday Morning with unabated eagerness to his compelling messages of varied interests, all leading to the same unchanging pleas for "man's humanity to Man." His scathing denunciation of injustice, his unfailing courage in the interpretation of his convictions, even to the point of inviting cruel unjust criticism from those who disagreed with him, carried me to look upon him as an undaunted defender of human rights. Actuated by the true spirit of comradeship, he never failed to lend his interest, his wise judgment and sympathetic co-operation whenever individual problems were brought to his attention, and I had the good fortune to be the recipient of his valuable services on needful occasions.

Words fail me, when I attempt to reveal the true impact of his great worth as a citizen of the world. I can only say that John Haynes Holmes, a beacon-light along-shore amid the moaning, surging tide of world conflict has ever inspired his fellow-beings with this hopeful outlook born of a faith that will not fail.—[from *Driftwood:*]

> O floating Spar of Hope
> Tis ours to cling full fast to thee,
> Outriding e'en the mighty wave
> And current, strong with black despair,
> Not even these have power to engulf,
> Nor stay thine onward course.
> Justice and Right are bearing down upon us
> Ay, holding out strong hands
> Of help and timely rescue,
> They lead to that long-looked for Haven
> Where man, at last plays fair with brother-man

And gives him back his ancient Right
Equality

## Mary Hall

Mary Hall possessed unusual physical beauty[,] a compelling personality, and a deep love for all humanity. Those clear blue eyes of hers seem to glow with a never-fading light of tenderness and sympathetic understanding.

I shall ever remember my first meeting with her. It was during the War-Camp Community activities, and I was assisting a Red Cross unit in the down-town district of Chicago, where she served as supervisor. After inspecting my work, she began conversing with me, and finally gave me a cordial invitation to visit her on the following evening, at which time she assured me that I would meet some very delightful friends. I did so, and, that occasion proved to be most enjoyable for the reason every one present seemed to be imbued with the spirit of brotherhood.

Mary Hall believed that we create a peaceful atmosphere within the four walls of our dwelling places by bringing together kindred souls. As a frequent guest in her home I was conscious of this soothing influence. I never wearied listening to the recital of her experiences in Europe, when as a Coloratura Soloist, she sang before royalty on many occasions. She inspired me with her expressions of unfailing belief in holding fast to one's ideals. For instance, at one time, she remarked, "Amid the fascinating life of Paris, I was gay, but I could never bring myself to lower the standard of high desire to serve my fellow-comrades. ["]

As a lover of poetry, she urged me to continue my efforts in that direction. One afternoon she asked me to read for her, one of my poetical compositions, entitled, The Great

Adventure, in which I had made known my belief in higher spiritual planes, where our earthly aspirations and longings would be happily fulfilled. She listened intently, her beautiful face beaming [?] with eager interest, and smilingly said— ["]I agree fully with you, Dear friend, and I want to you promise me that if I pass to those happy planes before you do, you will come and read this poem as a tribute to our friendship." I promised, two years later I was called to respond to that agreement, by her family, who had found this written request in her diary.

Somehow I have never felt that Mary Hall was really far away from me. I can only think of her as finding joyful satisfaction, upon the open plains of the

## The Great Adventure

### 1.

Down thro' the open windows
Of my Soul
Pours the changing glory
Of a Setting Sun;
And rays,
All crimson, gold and violet
Play with Aeolian sweetness
Across Life's memories,
Commingling, blending into perfect harmonies
The hours that I have known
In this—Life's passing Day

### 2.

And after crimson, gold and violet
Gave place to twilight
Soft and soothing twilight,
Lo, to my waiting soul
Comes down the calm of night
The closing of the day,
The promised Hour of Rest

3.

And then, behold, 'tis Morn
Freshness and fragrance everywhere!
From out the open windows of my Soul,
I gaze upon the glistening dew-drops
Of assurance,
Foretelling the endlessness of Immortality
Around me and beyond
Are fairest fields
Of rich fulfillment;
Above, plane after plane
Of rare attainment;
My dreams, at last,
Have ripened into
Blest realities
Here, in the long-looked-for Realm
Of Life supreme.

## On Bonnie Brae, Cape Cod, with Mrs. Lydia Weld

Bonnie Brae! even the thought of that beautiful hillside, stirs within me lasting memories of golden Autumn days in Falmouth, Cape Cod, Massachusetts, where I was companion to Mrs. Lydia Weld, an unmistakable aristocrat of German descent, who exemplified her knowledge of the fine art of living by her loyalty to high idealism. [S]he never lost an opportunity to give me a hopeful outlook on Life's changing affairs, which, in my later years, proved to be the fulfillment of her unfailing predictions.

I can clearly portray her sincere interest in me, by recalling one memorable Sunday Afternoon when we drove to her Camp Bonnie Brae, because, as she expressed it, "I desire to have you witness scenes from Nature that will make a lasting impression upon you, and reveal the larger meaning of Life's experiences."

After driving for some time, it was her wish that we leave our conveyance, and ascend, on foot, the rough, stony hillside. We did so, until we reached the summit overlooking one of the most inspiring scenes I have ever witnessed.

Before us, stretching far and away, were the sparkling waters of a clear, blue lake, bordered by multicolored wild flowers, while, just below us on one side of the banks, nestled Camp Bonnie Brae, half-hidden by tall stately trees. Before entering her log cabin, so obviously designed for rest and comfort, she turned to me and said so tenderly, "I shall rest for a while, but I have brought you here for a definite purpose. [. . .] The rough, stony hillside we have just climbed is an illustration of what Life may, at times, mean to you, and the unexpected scene of this beautiful lake, is a parallel to the brighter experiences you will yet enjoy: Now, for a brief while I want you to wander along the lakeside, drink in the fragrance of the wild flowers, and enjoy the grandeur of the scenery. ["]

I did, as she requested, deeply thrilled by the surrounding glory of a scene I shall ne'er forget.

When I returned to the Camp, she met me at the doorway, and smilingly said "now we shall take our homeward way, but, remember, some day, you will write of Bonnie Brae— not now—but in the calm years of your life."

After driving through the soft, Autumn twilight we reached her picturesque sea-side cottage, where she added to the joy of the day by reading choice selections from Rudyard Kipling's ["]Poems of the Sea."

One by one the Harbor lights gleamed forth, and, closing the book, she remarked, "These lights-along-shore, are happy illustrations of the friends who will come to you, one by one, in the years when you will need them most, and now 'good-night.'" I went to my rest, fully conscious of this benediction by a faithful friend, and it follows me even now, as I write of "Bonnie Brae" in these calmer years of my life.

Needless to say that having had the priceless privilege of nearness to such a rare friend, and the rich experience of the Autumn-glory on Bonnie Brae, I have cherished them as beacon-lights along the pathway of the years.

## Chapter 5
## HEIGHTS

### Sister Hurt

On the crest of a hillside road in Salem, Virginia, lived a beloved Cherokee Indian Friend of mine, known throughout the village as Sister Hurt, because of her hospitable attitude toward her fellow-beings. Her little dwelling was a veritable "House by the side of the Road[.]" Human beings of every known racial variety were welcome to rest beneath the shade of her little porch, and share with her whatever refreshment she had to offer. She was typically Indian in her phraseology, using few words, but her impressive silence was a convincing evidence of innate sincerity. She had her moments of meditation in a little sanctum just off her white-washed living-room, and it was my happy privilege to join her in the sacred silence of those hours. Little Odessa, a charming child of seven summers, adopted by Sister Hurt manifested the same spirit of hospitality toward all of Sister Hurt's guests. It was her great delight to scramble down the green hillside to the spring with her little tin pail, and bring up clear sparkling water to refresh a wayfarer. I shall never forget the joyous

expression on her radiant little face as she struggled up the
hillside one hot summer afternoon, her little pail running
over with the cooling draught as she called up to us in her
sweet childish voice, ["]See me coming—I'm coming up the
hill!" I have remembered those significant words all thro' the
years. They have often been a slogan to me when Life's way
had its upward trend, yes, a challenge and a clear clarion call
to journey even to the summit of seemingly insurmountable
difficulties.

Sister Hurt was a veritable "dweller on the heights" of
spiritual understanding, not only in her worship of Nature,
but also in her inspiring demonstration of loving fellowship
with those who needed courage and renewed faith to reach
the desired goal of worthwhile living. Each day that I spent
with her seemed like a lasting benediction even for the days
there were yet to come. I remember so clearly the end of one
perfect day, when, after leaving her I stood in the doorway
of another little home in Salem at the sunset hour, and reflected upon the golden glow of Sister Hurt's rare personality, and I could not resist expressing my deep appreciation
for her friendship in the following lines [from *Driftwood:*]

### At Sunset

1

I stood in the doorway at even
    And I looked to the hills far away,
Where the sun's last rays seemed to linger
    Ere they faded in brilliant display

2

Yes, lingered in beautiful splendor
    And the scene was rare to behold:
A pale blue sky was its background
    With stretches of pink and gold.

### 3

What wonder that Nature's rare beauty,
    So inspires the soul and thrills
Our beings with tender emotions
    As we look far away to the hills.

### 4

To the hills of which David has spoken
    "From whence comes my help," said he
And we have the same blest assurance
    As we gaze on their majesty.

### 5

And we think of the power that formed them,—
    They seem like a tower of defense
To protect and to ward off the evil
    Until we depart and go hence,

### 6

Where the sunlight fades not, but lingers
    and to-night my waiting soul thrills
As I stand in the doorway at even,
    Ad I look far away to the hills.

## Furman & Maye Fordham
## Music as a divine Art

There have been moments of inexpressible joy in my life when I have had the rich privilege of being very close to those rare interpreters of musical art, who seem to bear us aloft on wings of inspiration where we dream dreams of the attainable, even to untold Heights of Life's adventures.

Such has always been my experience under the subtle spell of Maye and Furman Fordham, lending their rich voices to eager listeners.

Furman was one of the finest vocal Instructors I have ever

known. Somehow he seemed to inspire his pupils with a yearning desire to make music, not only as prospective individual artists, but his choral groups caught the same spirit, as they sang in harmonious accord.

Maye breathed forth her rich Mezzo-Soprano tones with captivating sweetness and sureness, thrilling her audiences into breathless silence . . . always keeping in character with the theme of her chosen renditions.

I shall always remember her first Recital in Carnegie Chamber Music Hall, New York City. I seem always to recall her calm poised manner, as she stood beside the Steinway piano, a charming interpretation of rare personality.

Both Maye and Furman possessed the rare faculty of leading their listening audiences to exquisite heights of musical inspiration. My life has been greatly enriched by the friendship of these two artists who were so obviously endowed with the divine gift of Song[.]

## Dr. Zia Bagdadi

Among the numerous tokens of comradeship that I possess, there is one that seems always to lift me to a higher plane of living. It is an oxidized-framed square of parchment on which is inscribed the word "Allah." It was given to me as an evidence of genuine friendship by Dr. Zia Bagdadi, a fine Persian Idealist, who believed absolutely in Universal Brotherhood. On the back of this token, Dr. Bagdadi inscribed his name both in [A]rabic and [E]nglish, and upon presenting the gift he smilingly said "whenever you look at this word 'Allah,' you cannot fail to think of God, for such is its meaning."

I remember so well the summer afternoon in his strikingly beautiful home when as the guest of his wife, his daughter and himself, I was served a typical Persian dinner, and after drinking fragrant Oriental tea, we sat in restful silence while the gracious daughter softly chanted a Persian prayer that seemed to hover over us like a soothing benediction. It was also my privilege to visit the magnificent Bahai temple over-looking Lake Michigan on the shores of Wilmette, Ill., with Dr. Bagdadi and other kindred friends.

As I gazed upon the architectural beauty of the temple, its towering dome, and its arched entrances bespeaking welcome to all the nations of the earth, I could easily comprehend Dr. Bagdadi's devoted co-operation with the work of building a temple which in coming years would prove itself an open door to all humanity, regardless of circumstances or conditions.

Dr. Bagdadi was indeed a true and tried comrade, never failing to speak words of comfort and hope when weighty problems arose, and there was need for sympathetic understanding.

I am powerless to express what his friendship meant to me, the memory of which seems to surround me with the radiance of his high desire to render unstinted service in the spirit of universal love.

## John Greene, Baritone
## Chicago, Ill.

John Greene was one of the most interesting and understanding friends I have ever known. Running true to form, as an artist, he was temperamental to the last degree, but this characteristic was an attractive part of his personality.

I can never fully express what his friendship meant to me. He seemed to create the right sort of atmosphere for my enjoyment. Sometimes, it was an invitation to attend a Classical musicale, or a thrilling theatrical performance. Again we sought the haunts of bohemian life, where individuals expressed themselves freely and unreservedly in Art, and liberal attitudes toward their fellow-beings[.] Sometimes we took common fare in some obscure cafe—and revelled in the knowledge we ate where we wanted, to [be] utterly free from false social conventionalities. I remember one bitter cold day in Chicago, when my very soul seemed freezing within me, John said, ["]come with me, Olivia, let's dine together." And we proceeded to enter a small inconspicuous eating-place, where the food was good, and one would never encounter the would-be ultra individual who conformed only to the dictates of artificial society. After chatting merrily over our repast, in his keen discernment of my artistic needs, [he] invited me to spend the hours of his rehearsal with him, in the Studio of his fine accompanist, Theodore Taylor. I listened to song after song—rendered a richness and rare quality such as only the golden voice of John Greene could interpret. Somehow at the close of that bitter winter's day I felt that John had again played the part of true comradeship without obviously emphasizing his sincere desire to bring joy and comfort to a needy friend.

John was very young when he began his musical career, but he was destined to call forth high [unintelligible] of praise from the finest musical critics in our country. On one occasion when John was a guest in my little Studio, he sang for our visitors so delightfully that Mrs. Walter Hoffman[,] one of my German friends and a rare musical artist, exclaimed, "When John Greene sang I nearly passed out[,]" "he must be heard," and from that time on, she proceeded to arrange opportunities for concerts among the outstanding patrons of Art among the residents [of] Chicago's exclusive

North side. During these years, John has continued to achieve unequalled distinction in the realm of great-song-artists.

John Greene inspired me to write, in fact urged me to give expression to whatever was latent within me, and to him I owe my interpretation of "Shadows" the background of which I cannot refrain from making a part of this Narrative.

John in his determination to maintain a universal attitude toward his fellow-humans brought together a group of artistic friends, having their meeting-place on Indiana Ave. in a small, white-washed basement, known as "the Shadows[.]"

Here, we associated with every-known nationality[,] each one contributing his own interesting offering to programs that were as unique as they were varied. John insisted that I do something original in verse, and, altho I doubted my ability to create [a] worthwhile contribution, I felt that, as a member of the group, I must share whatever I had with them. I decided to attempt an imaginary portrayal of an early African civilization, when primitive life among its dwellers gave promise of inherited artistic potentialities, to be interpreted by future generations. Thus, in my imagination I asked of Life the mystic meanings of "shaded places" in the experience of those people of the early ages. Life's answer gave me the urge to write,

### Shadows

Life called insistently
["]Come, leave the glare
Of sun-lighted highways,"
Come where hidden recesses
Give pause and understanding.
I followed Life
Into the Shaded Places
And listened—etc

To me, John Greene and his Art is a striking illustration of inherited gifts, thro' which he is helping the world on right merrily, and for which his listeners all along the pathways will remain eternally grateful.

## Chapter 6
## FRAGRANT PATHWAYS

I once had a little flower-garden in the front yard of my childhood's home—11 D St. Providence Rhode Island[.]

In this garden there were tiny paths bordered with *Lillies-of-the-Valley*—the fragrance of which seemed always to overwhelm me with its delicate sweetness.

In the very heart of this city, bloomed a stately *Magnolia* tree, and its yearly appearance was another source of joy to my youthful years. With what childlike eagerness, I awaited its coming that I might again look upon its richly-tinted blossoms, and inhale their subtle fragrance.

Another memory of later years recalls my visit to friends in Danbury, Conn. where I spent many refreshing moments in the *flower-garden*—surrounded by roses of every hue, breathing forth unutterable sweetness, on the soft summer air. Damask red, shall-pin and snow-white roses, combined to paint a picture I can never forget.

The remembrance of these fragrances, are always associated with three rare comrades, whose very souls breathed forth continually the sweetness of universal love upon Life's pathways.

## Mary Hanaford Ford

Lillies of-the Valley to me are a fitting interpretation of dainty Mary Hanaford Ford, fragile and spiritual—tho' she was, and yet the possessor of strong spiritual magnetism, she seemed to enfold all who were permitted to come into her rare presence. Never have I known a soul that had such great capacity for inspiring fellow-beings with so deep a passion for genuine unity, exemplifying the true brotherhood of man. She was always deeply concerned in the best welfare of others, a loyal and unprejudiced contender for fair play, and an unfailing dispenser of loving kindness. I had the rich privilege of sharing sacred moments of meditation with her, in silent appeal to the Creator for needful blessings upon all humankind. Somehow, her frail physical presence, moving gently among us, seemed also to be living in some rarefied atmosphere just above this earth-plane. Often I felt like asking her the question I have clothed in verse,—

### *Whither?*

O Venturous Soul
Hast thou not kept
Thy winged way   etc.

Somehow, I feel that her holy quest for service divine, has never ended.

## Juliet Thompson

I cannot refrain from associating Juliet Thompson with the exquisitely-tinted flowers of the Magnolia tree. Her colorful personality, beauty of verbal expression, rare sense of humor, and warm-heartedness breathed forth rich fragrances all along the paths of life. Her affiliation with fellow-comrades from the Occident to the Orient, accounted for her versatility as a fascinating writer.

I cherish deeply the memories of my visits to her home in Greenwich Village where I listened to readings from her book, "The Magdalene," which revealed her native ability in the portrayal of human living. Her unusual interpretation of the high desire of "The Magdalene" in biblical story, thrilled me so completely that I could not resist writing my own conception of her inspired Theme, in rythmic form,—

### The Magdalene
(after listening to Juliet's inspired Theme)

Sadly, upon her Quest of Love
    E'en to Gethsemane she journeyed,
And gazing on His fearful agony,
    She breathed forth "O My Lord,
I love Thee—how I love Thee"
    and went her sorrowing way.

Now paused beside the sobbing Peter,
    Who moans "I have denied Him,
Woe is me! woe is me!"
    She whispers "Grieve thou not,
He knoweth well thy frame,
    And loves thee still."

On to the lonely place,
    Where Judas, the Remorseful One,
Cries out "Thou hatest me,
    I have betrayed the Prince of Peace."
She murmurs low "I hate thee not,
    For thou didst once bestow on me,
A sacred tress from the kingly head
    Of Christ, My Lord."

And now, her way
Leads to the foot of Calvary's Cross,
Where with aching, breaking heart
    She lies, prostrated,
Thro' all those anguished hours.
    Then rising, keeps her lonely,
Weary-watch—until the dawning
    Of a promised Morn.

'Tis dawn, at last!
   She gropes her way
Within the dark recesses
   Of a deserted Tomb,
Then out into a flower-scented field,
   With endless questioning—,
"Where hast thou lain My Lord?"

And now, a golden voice
   Calls gently "Mary"
While she, in rapture, all-divine
   Cries out, "O Master, My Beloved,"
And once again
   Her alabaster box of ointment,
Lies broken at His sacred feet.

             OLIVIA WARD BUSH-BANKS
             April 29, 1932.

Even as that glorious Magnolia tree heightened the joys of my childhood days, so the sweet, subtle influence of Juliet Thompson—has thrilled me with the consciousness of rare companionship, as I have met her again and again along the path of life and found myself refreshed by the fragrances of her compelling presence.

## Margarita Smythe

Damask, red, shell-pink, snow-white roses, and all the variegated beauty of a flower-garden are emblematic of Margarita's conception of fellow-humans. To her, physical varieties, were members of one great family, for which her ruling passion was that of unqualified love and unity.

    Margarita's home was uniquely interesting, having had at one time, as a distinguished guest, the late Abdul Baha, a great Bahai Teacher, whose spiritual influence seemed to permeate the quaint little dwelling at 48th W. 10th St. where

Margarita often called groups of comrades in loving unity. Indeed the whole aspect of these gatherings was like a veritable Rose-garden, representing all types of humanity in the varied coloring of many races. Margarita revelled in all of this, and often, on these occasions, as I looked upon her radiant countenance, she seemed like an ethereal being from some higher plane of existence, and I was constrained to visualize my beloved friend as one who constantly breathed in heavenly fragrances, and I feel the insistent urge within me to pay her this loving tribute

### Roses

Damask-red—shell-pink
And snow-white roses,
Enthrall me
With their subtle fragrance:
They speak to me of mystic things.

Can they be heralds
From the unseen Realm
Of Nature's paradise
Where Beauty's perfect pattern
Awaits the full release
Of earth-bound mortals?

O, that our souls
Might soar aloft
On fluttering wings
Of high-born vagrancy
And learn the cosmic secret
Of damask-red, shell pink,
And snow-white roses.

## Chapter 7
# SERENE VALLEYS

Among my fellow-travellers there have been those who, by their soothing influences, and calm serenity reminded me always of pleasant paths thro' quiet valleys. Ann Emanuel, one of my cherished comrades always poised, sincere and unwavering in her friendship was a striking illustration of quiet valleys. Her placid face with its rich brown coloring and nobility of expression never failed to impart the warmth of genuine welcome whenever I presented myself at the portals of her stately home on South Parkway—, Chicago, Ill. The best that she had to offer in fine hospitality was unstintingly mine. Her charm of manner and command of social graces were fascinating evidences of rich family inheritances. To be her guest was to revel in the refreshing atmosphere of kindred souls and delightful surroundings. How I loved to move slowly, down the broad winding staircase, past the rare old colonial clock in the Reception Hall, on into the drawing-room and sink luxuriously into the depths of a rich Oriental divan. Somehow, I felt that I must have known just such an experience in some former existence. As an artist, Ann brought to life the inspiring tompositions of rare old music masters, whenever her fingers moved deftly over the ivory keys of her magnificent instrument. Here I must also pay tribute to her companion, Harrison Emanuel[,] one of the Master-Violinists of the world, whose very soul spoke through the strings of his priceless Stradivarius. Listening to Harrison Emanuel, as, unconsciously he brought forth those magic strains in all his native genius, one felt as if the gifted artist was revealing the very presence of the music-masters of the Ages.

Harrison always accorded the same fine hospitality so tenderly extended by Ann.

[T]he late Francis Stradford, Sr., Ann's distinguished father, a dauntless defender of human justice and the highest standards of living, once said to me "hope this friendship between Ann and yourself will remain always the same." I rejoice to say that it has, throughout the years.

## Bertha Thomas

What a flood of memories surround me, when I recall the sunset hours spent in 35th St. Park, overlooking Lake Michigan, Chicago, Ill, where, as keen lovers of Nature one revelled in the beauty and calmness of those moments, awed into deep silence by the gorgeous coloring of a setting sun. We had so much in common, in Literature, Art, and the consideration of ethical vaues. In fact we both believed that our present existence was but a forecast of fulfilled ambitions and perfected ideas, to be realized fully, somehow, sometime, somewhere on future planes of living. We were not mere dreamers, far from it, because we knew full well, the varying circumstances of Life, and its constant demand upon unabated courage and determination to "carry on," as we went about our human business.

Bertha's physical background was unmistakably that of the commingled blood of numerous races, the Anglo-Saxon infusion being as convincingly dominant as her universal attitude toward her fellow-beings.

She possessed a delightful sense of humor to which I responded joyously in our observation of interesting types of humanity. Above all, her individuality and pronounced disregard of social conventions made our comradeship, a continued season of refreshing, like waters from valley springs.

How often, in the hurried life of turbulent New York City, I have longed for even a passing glimpse of that serene contenance, and to hear again, her re-assuring expressions of unfailing interest and sympathetic understanding in all that concerned me.

Again and again, in the yesteryears I have followed the lure of her unchanging belief in my powers of endurance, whenever I fared forth toward the attainment of cherished aims. She was indeed a devoted, dependable comrade in the onward trek of Life's affairs[.]

## Lee Rapaport

Little Lee (or Liba, meaning one that the people shall love) was of Russian descent. Her radiant face was always a source of spiritual uplift to me. There was ever the questioning look, as if in search of the mysterious unknown; or always asking the eternal question, Why?

Her greatest joy was that of discovering creative potentialities in little children, weaving around them delightful dream fancies in skillful dramatic imagery.

I have listened with delight to her interpretation of Jack and the Beanstalk, in which she obviously displayed an intriguing adaptability for creating unusual sequences in the development of her theme. She firmly believed that children of all racial varieties could be taught real love for humanity, through close contact, thereby creating a genuine understanding of real human values.

Lee inspired me by her thorough belief in my literary ability; indeed, she insisted upon my writing *The Lure of the [D]istances;* constantly challenging me to bring it is fulfillment: always reminding me of the urgent need for universal comradeship.

Whenever I think of Little Lee, and recall our pleasant comradeship, I seem to find myself soothed and comforted in the midst of perplexity, even as one feels the refreshing influence and serenity of quiet valleys, far removed from turbulence and confusion along Life's troubled trails.

## Dr. Badillo

Sometimes, along Life's pathway we touch personalities that leave a lasting impression upon us. I can never forget Dr. Badillo, a Mexican Indian, one of the rarest souls I have ever known. As a Dramatic Artist, he could not be equalled—so clearly and beautifully did he interpret Life thro' his Art. During one memorable summer at Atlantic City, N. J. it was my pleasant privilege to be his guest on numerous occasions when Dr. Badillo presented original Dramatizations at his unique Joy Theatre located by the ocean-side where one was refreshed by health-giving breezes from the waters of the Atlantic Ocean. He lived so fully in his art, that he never missed an opportunity to draw forth potential values in dramatic demonstrations.

One evening, while visiting his class, I saw him create a spontaneous interpretation of the legend of the Willow Plate, using his own conception of the romantic incidents woven around that well-known illustration of Oriental Life in far-off China. His natural adaptability for beautiful scenic effects was peculiarly thrilling in aspect. I recall vividly one of his Mexican scenes where moonlight seemed to flow over the mountain-peaks and later on, the darkened sky gave place to day-dawn in all the magic of its golden glow.

Dr. Badillo possessed a rare spiritual quality in his discernment of personalities, that enabled him to sound the depths of their longings and aspirations, and he never failed to follow up that recognition, with sympathetic understanding[,] maintaining always the encouraging attitude of comradeship towards his fellow-beings, whom he seemed ever to draw within his circle of fine friendship by his deep and sincere concern.

On the walls of my little Studio hangs an exquisitely wrought panel of feathered flowers and bright-colored birds, portraying the native art of the Mexican Indian, presented to me by Dr. Badillo on the eve of his departure to Mexico City, his beloved home-land. I prize this gift as an added token of his sincere friendliness and hearty good-will. Needless to say, that he fully recognized the nearness of seeming distances as one of the eternal verities leading us to a clearer conception of the true meaning of life.

# Chapter 8
# LAMPS AT EVEN

"And they shall light the lamps of love thereof, that they may give light on all the paths that lie ahead."

Diverging pathways often lead to open spaces. Thus, these intimate narratives reveal fine, contributive influences that have guided me happily over many winding trails to present years, and I am keenly conscious of the rich endowment of these golden memories, each one serving to illuminate the moments and hours of life as I live it to-day.

A retrospective survey of my experiences serves to deepen my gratitude to that wonderful aunt, Maria Draper, who laid sure foundaitons for my sojourn thro' the years, enabled me to develop a sense of values, by which I have discerned the nearness of human distances, and revelled in their delightful contacts.

And now, in the summing up of my appreciation for such loving beneficence [?], I pay fond tribute to my daughter,

Marie, and granddaughter Helen, who are proving themselves the "light of my days.["] Not only have they thoroughly understood my chosen interpretation of comradeship, they have also mainfested an encouraging, loving tolerance of my obvious departures from the beaten path of human preferment in the choice of companions.

As a child Marie gave evidence of a native aptitude for discerning values, and seeking solutions for perplexing problems. At eight years of age, she startled me with this question—["] Mother, where do our words go?["] I confess I was sorely puzzled, and admitted, with regret that I did not know. Doubtless, had the Radio and its seeming magic been in evidence as it is to-day, I would have resonded promptly "Our words are all around us, They go out on the air for miles and miles and are caught up by this marvelous instrument with its connecting vibrations, reaching the ears of people all over the world. There is no limit to their destinations.["]

On another occasion, little Marie stood beside me at the sunset hour, in West Medford, Mass, on the shore of the Mystic River, as we gathered fuel for our evening fire. She seemed to comprehend the expression on my face, as I watched the setting sun linger on Arlington Heights, the sparkling river between mossy banks, nestling cottages along shore, and, lastly upon a ruined bridge. She said, "Mother, you are going to write something." I did, and the *Boston Daily Transcript* printed it in its literary column. I called it—[from *Driftwood*]

### *"Fancies"*

> "[']Mid parted clouds, all silver-edged
>   A gleam of fiery gold;
> A dash of crimson-varied hues,
>   The sunset story's told.

A mirrored lake, 'tween mossy banks
 A lofty mountain ridge;
A cottage nestling in the vale,
 Seen from a ruined bridge.

A woman longing to discern
 Beyond the gleam of gold,
A rush of memory—a sigh;
 And Life's strange tale is told.

All thro' the years Marie has kept a steady faith in my creative impulses. Long before my narratives were fully rounded out, she expressed her unfailing belief and assurance as to my ability, in these hopeful, challenging words "Mother have you interviewed a possible publisher for *The Lure of the Distances* ?["]

Helen, my beloved granddaughter has manifested the same sweet confidence thus keeping alive the literary urge within me. Indeed she has been a veritable guiding light, when I have been in doubt as to what I should or should not publish in a future collection of *Driftwood*. I recall my saying to her at one time, "Helen if the opportunity comes for me to enlarge my book of poems, I shall not include certain verses because they have a sad strain running through them," Helen, immediately hurled forth this challenge—"Suppose Henry Wordsworth Longfellow had decided to omit his 'Rainy Day' or 'The Day is Done[,]' think what the world would have missed?" Needless to say I stood convicted.

When Helen read the opening declaration of my For[e]w[o]rd "Distances fascinate me," she exclaimed in her youthful enthusiasm, "O, I like those words, they thrill me! You must write *The Lure of the Distances*." It is needless to say that with this source of inspiration, I could not refrain from venturing forth upon such a quest.

It can be clearly seen that these near and dear ones, not

only find joy in my literary aspirations. They use every opportunity to surround me with artistic pleasures of life, such
as outstanding musical recitals, exhibitions of Art in painting, and historical programs of world-famed personalities.
Added to these, I am the recipient of every-day comforts,
unfailingly bestowed upon me. They persistently keep alive
my sense of humor which is undoubtedly a family inheritance, and a striking proof that we three have much in common. All that they do for me is a benediction, constraining
me to exclaim "Verily my lines have fallen in pleasant places,"
and light shines upon my ways.

Yes, these Lamps at Even send forth a steady glow, surrounding me with calm contentment, and in my closing word
to them and to all whose comradeship I have known, I dare
to hope that this effort to portray my ever-present desire for
loving unity may keep its tiny way, with, countless seekers,
towards the happy destination of human nearness and unbroken peace.

> The "distances" are nearer than we think
> And comrades true, are lighting up Life's trails
> And shining forth as "steady beacons"
> E'en to the "heights" of human venture;
> The "gleam and glow" of goodly fellowship
> Leads on o'er "fragrant pathways,"
> E'en thro' "vales serene"
> Where love, like "lamps at even"
> Sheds rays of calm contentment.

**FINIS**

# APPENDIX

## EXCERPT OF A LETTER FROM OLIVIA WARD BUSH [BANKS] TO ELLA WHEELER WILCOX *

For about fifteen years I have been desirous of publishing a collection of prose and verses, not that I feel in any great degree that they could ever be considered meritorious, but I have tasted the cup of human sorrow and disappointment, and I feel that I ought to be helpful to others for this very reason. I have called my collection *Driftwood,* because they are just "bits" of experiences cast up on the shore of my own life.

I have been, for the past seventeen years, sole provider for an aged aunt and two children. I have waited patiently for the opportunity to use whatever talent I may possess. While I am a colored woman, I feel strongly that I have by Divine direction been placed among my group of people for a specific purpose.

I love all things Oriental, and although I have experienced privations, yes, poverty, in all of its humilating forms, still when I find myself in the midst of luxurious surroundings, or breathing a cultured atmosphere I feel as if I am but

* In Wilcox, "Is She the Reincarnation of Queen Cleopatra?" *Boston American* (20 Oct. 1912), n.p. This and all subsequent letters in this Appendix are in The Bush-Banks Papers, Amistad Research Center, Tulane Univesity, New Orleans, LA.

renewing the experiences of some former period. My children are now able to care for themselves, the dear old aunt has passed into the "real life," and now my thoughts and energies are centered in the publishing of *Driftwood*.

Financially I am utterly handicapped, for the burdens of the years have left me bare of any means, but I believe that what I need is the renewal of "hopeful thoughts," which will eventually bring the material results. Will you kindly give me your best thoughts for the needs of my life?

I love all things of earth. I am glad for the beauty and strength of the hills and flowers, and in them all, I find the Creator!

Happily I have had the privilege of being keenly alive to the amusing side of life, and have the love of many friends, and even though all the years of my life I have felt "lonely amid the multitude," still you will understand when I say I am "glad for life."

What I need is to be strengthened mentally: I have let go my hold somehow on the hopefulness of former days; I have lost my way, and so out of my heart I write to one who understands. I have had some little experience as a public speaker, and while I shrink from publicity, still I feel that I have a message.

Oh, I am so heart-hungry for mental encouragement, I need your strength, and again I ask you to give me your best thoughts for my heart's desire.

OLIV[IA]E WARD BUSH [BANKS]
932 Tremont St., Boston, Mass.

# AUTOBIOGRAPHICAL STATEMENT*

I, Olivia Ward, the daughter of Abraham and Eliza Ward, was born on the twenty-seventh day of February, 1869, in the little village of Sag Harbor, Long Island, in the state of New York.

I seemed to have lost my identity regarding the distinctness of race, being of African and Indian descent. Both parents possessed some negro blood, and were also descendants of the Montauk tribe of Indians, which tribe formerly occupied the eastern end of Long Island known as Montauk.

At the age of nine months I was left motherless, and my father then came with his three small chidren to Providence. In two years' time he married again; family difficulties arose regarding the children, and as a result I came under the guardianship of my aunt, my mother's sister, by the name of Maria [pronounced Mo-ri-a] Draper, who willingly assumed the responsibility of training me, and here began for her, a life of sacrifice which lasted from my childhood to womanhood.

My aunt was a woman of rare instinctiveness, and extraordinarily keen perceptibilities, possessing a great determination of purpose, and in hardships displaying that stoical endurance which so fittingly characterizes the nature of the Indian.

From early childhood, her lifework seems to have been, to sacrifice for others; owing to this she was unable to secure an education, which privilege denied, seemed but to strengthen

---

*Manuscript (c. 1914), opposite front. in Olivia Ward Bush [-Banks], *Driftwood*. Reproduced by courtesy of Collection of American Poetry and Plays, John Hay Library, Brown University, Providence, RI.

her efforts to prepare me for a higher station in life than had been her lot to fulfill.

Through her efforts I have secured a useful, practical education, and firmy believe that whatever I have attained . . . is due to her untiring zeal and loving interest in my welfare. She also exercised that same zeal and interest throughout that portion of my life which proved most extremely unfortunate.

At the age of twenty I married Frank Bush; domestic misfortune followed; and I found myself a young woman left with the sole responsibility of two little ones; who I am making strenuous efforts to support.

At this period of my life I acted upon my natural inclination toward literary work which as a child I had been deeply interested in, particularly poetry which seems always to have impressed me most peculiarly.

It may be, that physical suffering, extreme adversity and misfortune, have aided me in this work in that they have aroused the latent desires and ambitions which otherwise might not have been realized.

Sensible of the fact that the pecuniary results of my work is of much-needed personal benefit to me, I am also fully conscious, that it will, in however small a degree, tend toward the uplifting of the dark-skinned race, known as the colored people of America, among whom I am identified and who at the present day feel so keenly the pangs of prejudice and injustice. To me this thought alone serves as an inspiration.

And lastly, let me say that if humanity, in whatever condition it may be, is helped by one thought or word of mine, I shall feel conscious of having attained unto a long-desired end.

OLIVIA WARD BUSH

# LETTER FROM DOROTHY BALDWIN AND MAURICE BEEKER TO OLIVIA WARD BUSH-BANKS

Phone—
0092 Academy

383 Central Park W.
Nov. 25, 1930

Dear Olivia Ward Bush-Banks:

We are very sorry indeed to hear that you are no longer to function as Director of the International Poetry Group.

Is it possible that your withdrawal from that very interesting circle means its dissolution? We hope not—We also look forward to meeting you again at their gatherings should there be any in the future.

We have always enjoyed their general hospitality & have felt that a great deal of the success of those evenings were due to your very charming presence & your directing genius.

With best wishes and fondest regards, believe us

Very Sincerely yours

Dorothy Baldwin
Maurice Beeker

P.S. It will be sad news indeed to pass on to our friends.

# LETTER FROM OLIVIA WARD
# BUSH-BANKS TO N. R. STANTLEY

Tel. New Rochelle 8778

57 Morris St. (apt. I.)
New Rochelle, N.Y.
July 25, 1932

Mr. N. R. Stantley,
Radio Station W.A.A.T.
Jersey City, N.J.

My Dear Mr. Stantley;

In keeping with my promise, I am enclosing the poem you liked "Filled with You," and several others. Please accept my apology for the copy of "Aunt Viney Sketches.["] I could not find the neat copy, but I wanted to send it at this writing. I have already twelve Aunt Viney sketches, in which Aunt Viney has various humorous experiences.

All of the material I have used in these sketches have been taken from that which I have actually seen and heard from different individuals in the colored group. I feel safe in letting you see them, because I know that you appreciate and recognize their origin.

You may keep all that I have sent you, and after I hear from you, I will send you a more presentable copy of the Sketch.

Awaiting your reply to the value of the Sketch, I am,

Cordiall[y] yours,

# LETTER FROM JOHN GREENE
# TO OLIVIA WARD BUSH-BANKS

Saturday night, Oct. 30th

Darling Olivia:

How in this ugly, dissatisfied old world, can you find such beauty and write so beautifully of it? It proves so much— your artistry, your fine womanhood, your optimistic outlook on life and your tender soul. I wish that I could be like you and I believe your letter, poem, etc., will help me. Since it came I have, in a measure forgotten or refused to recognize many of the ugly spots before me, such as unemployment, frayed shirts, thin soles on my scuffed shoes, and shiny suits. Instead, I can see the beautiful personality and friendship of Dr. Reese, the wonderful work going on here at Lincoln Centre, and the integral part that Dr. Reese is permitting me to play in it.

Imagine Olivia, thirty and more eager children, some with bright shiny faces and some pale and lined. They are all looking up at me, smiling, and I am teaching them to sing— Do they sing? Ah, you should hear my children.

Can you see me Olivia, on Sunday mornings here? I am the choir of Dr. Reese's new church, the whole choir, just me alone. All eyes are on me and all ears are open to my song. Yes darling Olivia, I do believe I am happy since receiving your letter, poem, etc. You will send more, won't you?

I am so happy to hear from you, I thought I had lost you

and I was so sad. Remember, you are the greatest inspiration that I have, you will continue to be, won't you?

Always,

John Greene
Lincoln Centre
700 Oakwood Blvd.
[Chicago]

# LETTER FROM CARTER G. WOODSON TO OLIVIA WARD BUSH-BANKS

## THE ASSOCIATION FOR THE STUDY OF NEGRO LIFE AND HISTORY, INCORPORATED

Washington, D.C.
December 22, 1938

Mrs. Olivia Ward Bush-Banks,
214 West 128th Street,
New York City

My dear Mrs. Banks:

I have received your poetry and I like it very much. In some issue of the NEGRO HISTORY BULLETIN I should like to make use of one or more of these poems. We have nothing that we can give you in way of compensation but what we may return in kind. This is a struggling cause and it cannot pay for contributions.

Thanking you for your interest, I am

Respectfully yours,

C. G. Woodson,
Director

# NOTATION ON THE CREATION OF AN ART GROUP

An interesting Art Group came into being in the Studio of Olivia Ward Bush-Banks, Dramatist and Author, 2352-7th Ave. Friday Eve., Nov. 15, 1940.

Mrs. Bush-Banks, the promoter is widely-known for her deep interest in creative and artistic expression[,] firmly believing in the comradeship of co-operation in the field of varied arts.

Among those present, representing music, drama, painting, and scientific artistry were,

Ann Stradford Emanuel, noted Concert Pianist, Dorothy Dent, painter in Oriental Art, Will Anthony Madden, founder and director of the Greenwich Village Studio Theatre, Florence Willis, patron of Oriental Dance Groups, Leon Devan, of Assyria, Scientist in the art of an advanced system of lighting, demonstrating alternate light and shadow effects, Lee Rapoport, Creative Drama director.

The Art Group is arranging for an evening in the near future at the Stratford-Emanuel Music Studios, in Hotel Theresa, 125th & 7th Ave.

# ENTRIES FOR A PROJECTED JOURNAL

Christmas Day
Thursday, December 25, 1941

Spent day with my loved ones, Marie and Helen at 4854 W. 138th Str., Apt. 16c.

Helen cooked dinner, Marie was convalesing from a month's illness. Thank God she was able to be walking around and assist in a small way. The little home was so attractive and cheery with its lighted fireplace, and the beautiful plants, poinsettias and others sent by the nurses, also a multitude of beautiful cards, and the lighted candles burning while we listened to the radio's glorious Christmas music. I received lovely gifts from Helen and Marie and the whole atmosphere was filled with love: What a day! I kept praying within, that Marie and I would be greatly improved in health and continue to believe in His words, "All things are possible to him that believeth." Prayer changes things. Thank God for a glorious Christmas Day with those so near and dear to me. (Another Year)

Christmas Day
Friday, December 25, 1942

Spent day with my loves ones, Marie and Helen at our Harlem Health Food Center, 104 W. 124th Street. Marie cooked dinner (delicious meat substitute with gravy, yams, white potatoes, cranberry sauce, carrots, apple pie). Little Toto, Helen's pet cat, had his Xmas gift (an artificial mouse filled with catnip), which delighted him greatly. Marie had tried her gift on Toto (a bright Christmas ribbon). Marie said to me, with grateful tears in her eyes, she was so glad to have me with them. Also that they did not expect to have me with Helen and she as a member of Ephesus S.D.A. [Seventh Day Adventist Church.] It made us all so happy. Helen distributed the gifts. To Marie, a nice bathrobe from Helen, and a warm blue nightdress from Mama. To Helen, a cream colored silk blouse made by Sweetheart [Bush-Banks's nickname], and a corduroy shirt made by Marie. To myself, a lovely Christmas Home Calender and morning watch from

Helen and Marie, also a pretty new dress (black crepe, buttoned down the front, trimmed with Indian colors, on collar, and Indian-colored pockets). Marie was better in health, and I was able to walk and eat heartily. God has really blessed me with reasonable health. Thank God for one more Christmas day with my loved ones. Anthony [Banks] sent money for Christmas from Chicago. So ended a happy Christmas tide.

OLIVIA WARD BUSH (BANKS)
2352 7th Avenue
[New York]